NEWSPAPER EXCERPTS FROM

The Maysville Eagle

MASON COUNTY KENTUCKY

1827-1847

Rachelle Winters-Ibrahim

HERITAGE BOOKS
2007

HERITAGE BOOKS
AN IMPRINT OF HERITAGE BOOKS, INC.

Books, CDs, and more—Worldwide

For our listing of thousands of titles see our website at
www.HeritageBooks.com

Published 2007 by
HERITAGE BOOKS, INC.
Publishing Division
65 East Main Street
Westminster, Maryland 21157-5026

Copyright © 2007 Rachelle Winters-Ibrahim

Other books by the author:

Excerpts from the Earliest Mason County, Kentucky Newspapers: The Mirror, 1799 (May 31; June 14 and 28; July 5, 10, 17 and 24; August 7-28; September 4-25; October 9-30; and November 6, 17 and 20) and The Maysville Eagle, 1818 (July 15 and September 17) and 1825 (March 16 and 23)

All rights reserved. No part of this book may be reproduced or transmitted in any form or by any means, electronic or mechanical, including photocopying, recording or by any information storage and retrieval system without written permission from the author, except for the inclusion of brief quotations in a review.

International Standard Book Number: 978-0-7884-3648-2

As always, to my father, Robert L. Winters; my husband and children; my sister, Linda Easter; and brother, Bob Winters. In memory of my mother, Mildred Wheadon Winters; my brother, Michael McClanahan; and my sister, Sharon Gibson.

Foreword

These *Maysville Eagle* excerpts were taken from the 1827-1867 film. All of the earliest issues are included between the years 1827 and 1846 that were found on the film. Issues included: Saturday, January 10, 1846; Saturday, December 27, 1846; Wednesday, October 16, 1844; March 27, 1844; August 14, 1841; November 29, 1837; Wednesday, July 18, 1827; July 11, 1827; May 23, 1827; and March 28, 1827. The date on the bottom of most entries was from the printer. The dates indicated the first date that the article ran in the newspaper.

Some of the issues were damaged and, when the print was not legible, I inserted a "?" for a word and "...." for words that were missing.

Politics took up a major portion of the newspaper and I would advise anyone who is interested in an ancestor that served during the time period to read the articles for themselves. I did not include their names in the book because most entries were "how did they vote" on different bills. The political articles included on the film were very interesting. I would advise anyone who is interested in the Civil War to read these papers. As early as 1827, you get a hint of anti-slavery sentiment which continued to blossom. Political rivalry was enormous during this time and strong feelings on both sides prevailed.

The Maysville Eagle

The Maysville Eagle, Maysville Ky. Wednesday, March 28, 1827.

Printed and Published by Lewis Collins, Market Street, Maysville. Terms for one year, payment in advance, $2.50. For one year, payment within the year 8.00. For six months, in advance 1.50. Terms of advertising. 16 lines, or under, three insertions, $1.00, Each additional insertion, .25 The same by year, 10.00.

The following gentlemen are requested and authorized to act as agents, in receiving and forwarding monies due this establishment and procuring subscribers. They are solicited as an act of kindness, to receive no subscriber who is not both able and willing to pay punctually. Mayslick, Asa R. Runyon, P. M. Germantown, Ludwell Owens, P.M. Clarksburg Wm. S. Parker, P. M. Vanceburg, Benjamin F. Holton. Flemingsburg, A.E. Ballard, P. M. Carlisle, Joseph F. Tureman. Greenupsburg, Dr. H. E. Green, P. M. Augusta , Samuel Boud, P. M. Falmouth, R.A. Collins, Williamstown, James Collins.

Historical. From the Kentucky Gazette. Notes on Kentucky. Section XXVIII. The convention that met on the 8th of Aug. 1785, recommended it to the officers of the militia to meet in their respective counties and adopt such plans as should be deemed most expedient for the protection and defense of the country. To effect this end an expedition was set on foot against the Wabash Indians, who were at that time considered the most troublesome, and the command given to Gen. Clarke. About one thousand men were soon raised who rendezvoused at the Falls of Ohio, and from thence marched towards the Indian towns. In consequence of the delay in the boats which were to take the provisions up the Wabash, as well from the scarcity of provisions, the men when within two days march of the Indian towns became mutinous, upon which Gen. Clarke called a council of his officers; they were rather tofruituous, and they therefore concluded to return home.
After crossing the Ohio River, Col. Benjamin Logan returned to Kentucky, for the purpose of raising a party to march against the Shawnee Indians who lived on the Scioto. It was expected that the attention of these Indians would be attracted by the march of Gen. Clarke to the Wabash, and that their towns would be left defenseless. To accomplish this over a week elapsed before Col. Logan crossed the Ohio with his forces. As was expected, Col. Logan surprised an Indian town, killing several worriers and took many woman and children prisoners.

The Maysville Eagle

During this year (1785) frequent intelligence was received of the hostile designs, machinations and warlike preparations of the Indians. But they were not actually very troublesome. To the nations north of the Ohio, overtures of peace had been made by the general government, and Gen. Clarke with Gen. Parsons, from New England, and Gen. Butler from Pennsylvania, attended as commissioners at the mouth of the Great Miami in September or October, but they were met by no tribe except the Shawnees, and even as to them the meeting answered no beneficial purpose. It is true that they entered into a treaty in the January following, but did it in such a manner as afforded reason to believe that they would not abide by it and their future conduct confirmed the apprehensions then entertained. Gen. Butler was agent in behalf of the United States for Indian affairs, and as a Pennsylvanian, had no favorable impression for the Virginia character. Gen. Parsons, in all probability had no small share of that strong aversion which his countrymen have uniformly manifested towards the people of Virginia. Certain it is, that they both entertained great prejudices against the Kentuckians, and Gen. Butler represented them to Congress as the aggressors and fostered the sentiment then but too readily entertained by that body, that to the white people of the western county, and not the Indians, out the continuation of hostility to be inputed.

....

Miscellaneous. From the Philadelphia Album. The Martyr, an Historical Tale. By James J. Brownlee, of New York. A very lengthy story in two parts of Sir James Stewart a staunch Whig who braved the tyranny of Charles the Second.

Colonization Society. At the annual meeting of the Berkley County Auxiliary Colonization Society, held at Martinsburg, Va. On the 22 February, at which Dr. Thomas Davis delivered a very able and interesting address.

In reply to the call, contained in this paper of the 14th instant, by a number of the citizens of Lewis, we have received the following note from William B. Parker, Esq. Mr. Collins: Sir - You will please to inform the citizens of Lewis County, through the medium of your useful paper, that I have consented to run as a candidate for the legislature, although I had much rather run after an old buck in the Kinney Hills. Yours respectfully, Wm. B. Parker.

Virginia Senator Tyler. A public dinner was give at Richmond, on the 3d inst. To Governor Tyler at his retirement form the Chief Magistracy of the state of Virginia. A two column toast was published.

The Maysville Eagle

Dinner to Mr. Randolph. Mr. Randolph, the sage of Roanoke, had a public dinner given him by his political and personal friends, at Richmond, on the 10th inst. A full column toast was published.

Death. In Flemingsburg, on Thursday, the 22d inst. George W. Botts, Esq. A valuable citizen of that place.

Bracken Circuit March Term 1827. The President & Directors of the Bank of the Commonwealth, complainants vs. Eli Tucker & others, defendants The defendants, William Helm, Thomas Helm, Samuel Helm, Merideth Helm, and the heirs of Merideth Helm, deceased and the heirs of Charles Ford, whose names are unknown, not having entered their appearance herein, agreeably to law and the rules of the court, and it appearing to the satisfaction of the court that they are not inhabitants of this commonwealth: Upon the motion of the complainant, it is ordered that they appear here on or before the first day of the next June term of this court, and answer the complainants bill, or the same will be taken for confessed and that a copy of this order be published in some authorized newspaper of Kentucky for two months successively. A copy Attest, John Payne, C.B.C.C.

Spring and Summer Goods. Sumrall & Adams, have just received and are now opening at their store, corner of Water and Main Cross streets, a large and very choice assortment of seasonable goods, which they will sell very low for cash or approved country produce. Their friends and customers, and all others who would make a judicious expenditure for their money, are solicited to call and examine for themselves. Maysville, March 28.

Milliner Business. The subscriber has commenced the above business, both in Silk & Leghorn, in the town of Washington, Ky. in the house at the extreme North end of Main street, on the East side of the street, where she will execute all work committed to her trust, in the neatest manner, and at the shortest notice - and she hopes by assiduous attention to business, to merit a share of the Public patronage. Mary Brown. March 21, 1827.

Theatre . On Monday Evening, 2b April, the Maysville Thespian Society will perform Morton's celebrated comedy, called Education, and the laughable farce of the Bee Hive. For particulars, see bills.

Partially cut ad. seph M'Gallaird, now occupied by Edward Moore. The sale will be on a credit of two years, the purchaser giving bond with

The Maysville Eagle

sufficient security for the payment of the purchase money. Charles Humphreys, Com'r March 21, 1827

Information Wanted. Having important business with a man by the name of John Paxton, who once resided in Maryland, Allegany county and who now, it is believed, resides somewhere in the state of Kentucky, intelligence of his place of abode is most respectfully solicited. Said Paxton will probably know me when he hears my name. If this should meet his eye, he will be pleased address me at Maysville, Ky. where I shall remain for a few... I will give a reward of $5 ... ense a friend may be at to hear .. John Paxton ..... said Paxton is a witness in an important case. Dennis B. Hoblitzell Near Cumberland, Allegany county, March 21, 1827

Strayed, from the farm of Daniel Perrine, in Mason County, living on the road leading from Washington to Anderson's Ferry, on the 9th instant. A Bay Horse, rising four years old, has a start and snip, three white feet; had received a wound on the knee of the right fore leg, the swelling of which had not entirely abated when he left the place aforesaid: the hair worn off his sides by the skirts of the saddle. It is supposed that he will make for some of the southern counties, probably Madison. Any person taking up said horse, and delivering him at the place from he eloped, or to the subscriber at Perrine & Pickett's mill, on Lawrence's creek, shall be liberally rewarded G. Perrine. March 14.

State of Kentucky, Mason County, Sct. February Court 1827. Daniel Jenkins & Overton Jenkins, Appellants - against Presley Gill, agent for William Phillips' heirs, Appellee. Upon an appeal from the judgment of Rich. Soward, Esq. The defendant not having entered his appearance herein, agreeably to law and it appearing to the satisfaction of the court that he is not an inhabitant of the state; upon motion of the appellants, by their attorney. It is ordered that unless said appellees shall appear before the justices of the county court of Mason county, on the second Monday in May next, and answer the said appellee, the service of process shall be taken as confessed and that a copy of this order be published in some authorized newspaper for two months in succession.

The undersigned offer for sale, the Maysville Steam Oil Mill. This establishment is capable of making 40 gallons of linseed oil per day. With it is connected a Flour mill, capable of manufacturing 24 barrels of flour per day. The establishment is conveniently situated on Water Street, for receiving from and discharging into boats. For the obtaining of Flax seed, no place exceeds it, as it is bro't to this market a great distance by water, and from the states of Ohio & Kentucky by land. The great road crossing

The Maysville Eagle

these states passes here; and as persons wishing to purchase, will view the advantages for themselves, no other description is necessary. Geo & Amos Corwine. Maysville, Jan. 3, 1827.

Eagle Tavern, Washington, Kentucky. Joseph H. Hudnut. Respectfully informs his friends and the public, that he has taken the large brick building on Main Street, Washington, (heretofore occupied by Capt. B.B. Stith) Where he is prepared to accommodate travelers and others who may favor him with their custom, in a manner which he trusts, cannot fail to render general satisfaction. Pledging himself to use every exertion to promote the comfort of his customers, he respectfully solicits a portion of public patronage. Washington, Feb. 14, 1827.

Apprentices to the Blacksmith Business. Two youths, of industrious habits and of good moral character, between the ages of 15 and 17 years, will be taken as apprentices to the Blacksmith Business on application to the subscriber. Living on the road from Maysville to Mayslick, one mile north east of the latter place. John T. Waddell

Books, Edward Cox, Has lately received a supply of New and standard books, an addition to his former stock, which are offered for sale at the lowest prices. A long list of books available. Cash, Books or paper for Rages. Maysville, March 14.

Blacksmithing. The subscriber begs leave to inform his friends and the public generally, that he has rented the Blacksmith Shop in Maysville, formerly occupied by Richard Dement, on Second Street, nearly opposite the Methodist meeting house, where he means to carry on his business in the various branches. Every attention will be paid to customers and as he is determined to give the strictest attention to his business he hopes to receive a share of the public patronage. He intends to continue manufacturing the Patent Balance Scale Beams. John Jack. Maysville Feb. 21, 1827

Boot & Shoe Making. Grant & Campbell, respectfully inform their friends and the public in general, that they have taken the house lately occupied by George Cox, as a store room a few doors above Capt. Langhorne's tavern, on Front street, where they will keep constantly on hand, and are prepared to make on the shortest notice, Gentlemen's calf skin and Morocco boots & shoes, of the best materials, and not inferior in point of workmanship to any made at the Eastward. Maysville, March 7

The Maysville Eagle

Commissioner's Sale. By virtue of a decree of the Mason circuit court, made at the February term, 1826, in favor of Michael Wilson against John John and others, I shall, on Friday the 6th day of April next, proceed to sell on the premises. The tract of land mentioned in said decree, situate on the head of Bull Creek, Mason County, to the highest bidder, on a credit of two years, the purchaser giving bond with sufficient security for the purchase money. The sale will commence between the hours of 10 o'clock a.m. and 2 o'clock p.m. Winslow Parker, Com'r. March 7, 1827.

To Farmers. Those persons who are in want of ploughs, and are willing to give me eight dollars for first rate two horse ploughs, with cast iron mould boards will call or send to my shop and get them - try them fifteen days, and if they should not prove as represented, return them from whence they came, and your money shall be refunded. I have ploughed and made ploughs for nearly thirty years, and with that experience I am stimulated to recommend them as amongst the most valuable and least liable to get one of order that have been offered to the farmers within my recollection. They will be sent to most of the neighboring towns where they can be seen and had by applying. D. Lindsay. Maysville, March 7.

Twenty Dollars Reward. Strayed or stolen from the subscriber, living at Poplar Plains, Fleming County, Kentucky. Four horse beasts. They broke or were..... on Wednesday night the 14th inst. The following is a description of them. 1 large bright sorrel Horse well made to his size, no brand or mark perceivable. One pale Sorrel colt, two years old, blaze in his face, hind feet white, very large of his age. One bright bay mare, 3 years old past, hind feet white. One chestnut sorrel mare, getting in years, no mark or band perceivable. The colt is shod before and the others all round - all natural trotters. Any person delivering said horses to me, shall receive the above reward. Will. Pearce. February 28, 1827.

Horse-Wheel for sale. I wish to sell the horse wheel and drum which have been attached to my cotton factory. The cog wheel is eighteen feet in diameter, the horse walk twenty-eight, and from the proportion, it has run the lightest and with the least power of any wheel I ever saw. I will sell it very low. Val. Peers. Maysville, 6th March 1827.

Public Sale. Will be offered at Public Sale on Thursday, the 5th of April next, at the late residence of Alexander Dougherty, deceased, in Mason County, all the personal estate of said decedent, consisting of Four likely Negroes, one man, one boy and two women; horses, cattle, hogs, sheep, household & kitchen furniture, farming utensils; two road wagons, one

The Maysville Eagle

Dearborn wagon, ten sets of geer and a quantity of leather. Sale to commence at 10o'clock, a.m. and continue from day to day until all the property is sold. Twelve months' credit will be given on all sums over five dollars. The purchaser giving bond with approved security - on sums of five dollars and under, cash in hand will be required. Thos. M. Dougherty, Ex'or. March 14, 1827. All persons indebted to the estate are requested to come forward and settle and those having claims will please present them, properly authenticated. T.M.D.

Doct. Shackleford, Continues the practice of Medicine in Maysville. He may at all times be found, unless absent on professional business, at his office, on Second Street, two doors below the late Bank of Limestone, or at his dwelling on Second Street, in Armstrong's Row. Maysville, April 5, 1826

Wm. S. Bodley, Will practice law in the courts of Mason, Fleming and Lewis counties. His office is in Maysville, on Front Street next door below Mr. John Roe's. Maysville, March 14, 1827.

Weaving. The subscriber respectfully informs his friends and the public generally, that he has commenced the above business in Washington, at the Bagging factory of Mr. J.C. Dewees, where he will weave, coverlets, counterpanes, carpeting, table linen, janes, linsey, broadcloth, cassinet, blanketing, flannel & c. & c. In the best manner, and upon unusually low terms. From his experience and attention to business, he hopes to receive a share of public patronage. Isaiah Thompson. Feb. 14, 1827

Doctor Nelson, has returned to Maysville, and has the pleasure of informing his friends that he is disposed henceforward to be perfectly satisfied with the dull pursuits of private life, and that he has determined to devote his whole time and attention to the practice of medicine. His shop is on Second Street, where he may always be found, except when absent on professional business. Maysville, January 31, 1826.

Livery Stable The subscriber has opened a livery stable, on Sutton Street, Maysville, where he will keep horses by the week or otherwise, on as good terms as any other person in the place. Having an experienced man to take charge of his stable, he hopes to share a part of the public patronage, as every attention that is necessary will be paid to horses taken in charge. He also intends keeping a few horses for hire, & c. Wm. Murphy. Maysville, July 26

The Maysville Eagle

Flour. We have just received a few hundred bbls. Family Flour, of choice brands, from Zanesville, Ohio, warranted entirely clear of weevil, which we will retail in this market. Also 1 sack of wheeling hops, with which we will accommodate country distillers. We will give cash for 500 bushels corn. Hixson, Morton & Hixson. Maysville, March 14, 1827

Bank of Limestone. The President and directors of the Bank of Limestone, have given the undersigned a general agency for the purpose of closing the business of that institution. It will, therefore, be expected that the debtors to the bank (the most of whom have been furnished with a statement of their accounts) will make arrangements for the payment of the balances due. As it is absolutely necessary that the business should be closed as speedily as possible, it is believed that no debtor to the institution will feel himself exempted from this call. Wm. B. Phillips, Agent, Maysville, Feb. 1 1826

January & Huston, have just received at their commission house the following articles. Long list of articles. All of which they will sell low for cash or barter for feathers, hemp, leaf tobacco, ginseng, beeswax, Rags & c. Maysville, March 21, 1826

Tailoring. Aaron Quinn respectfully informs his friends and the public, that he has returned to Maysville, and taken his old shop on Water Street, next door above Mrs. Carrell's tavern, where he is prepared to execute all orders in his line with neatness and dispatch. He solicits the public patronage, Maysville, Nov. 15.

Richard Henry Lee, will practice law in the circuit and county courts of Mason and in the Bracken, Fleming and Lewis Circuit Courts. He keeps his office a few doors above Capt. M. Langhorne's Hotel, in the room lately occupied by Edward Cox as a Book Store. Maysville, May 3rd, 1826.

Putty. The subscriber keeps a constant supply of superior putty for sale low for cash. Isaac Qutten. N. B. He also keeps boat pumps of the best quality, constantly on hand for sale, very low for cash. Maysville, Oct. 11

La Mott's Cough Drops. Important medicine for coughs and consumptions. This elixir is not offered to the public as infallible, and a rival to all others, but as possessing virtues peculiarly adapted to the present prevailing disorders of the breast and lungs, leading to consumption. A timely use of these drops may be considered a certain cure in most cases of common colds, coughs, influenza, whooping cough, pains in the side, difficulty of

The Maysville Eagle

breathing, want of sleep arising from debility, and in spasmodic asthma it is singularly efficacious. A particular attention to the directions accompanying each bottle is necessary. The following certificates from respectable gentlemen, physicians and surgeons, are subjoined, to show that this composition is one which enlightened men are disposed to regard as efficacious and worthy of public patronage. Having examined the composition of Mr. Crosby's improvement upon La Mott's Cough Drops, we have no hesitation in recommending them to the public, as being well adapted to those cases of disease for which he recommends it. Doct's Jona. Dorr, dated Albany, Dec. 4, 1824; James Post, of White-Creek, Feb. 14, 1825, Watson Sumner and Jno. Webb, M.D. of Cambridge, Feb. 20, 1825. Solomon Dean of Jackson, Jan. 20, 1825. Mr. A. Crosby, I am pleased with this opportunity of relating a few facts, which may serve in commendation of your excellent cough drops. For ten years I was afflicted with a pulmonary complaint, my cough was severe, my appetite weak, and my strength failing. I used many popular medicines but only found temporary relief, until by a continued use of your valuable drops, I have been blessed with such perfect health as to render further means unnecessary. Ebenezer Harris. Salem (N.Y.) Jan. 12th 1825. Prepared by O & S Crosby, (Columbus, O.) whose signature will be affixed in their own hand writing to each bill on directions. Be particular that each bottle is enveloped in a stero or check label, which is struck on the same bill with the directions. Sold wholesale and retail by them and agents of their appointing throughout the United States and the Canada's; and by special appointment at the drug store of Dr. Coburn, Maysville. Each bottle contains 45 doses; Price one dollar single; nine dollars per dozen.

New Goods, James Morrison & Co. Have just received and are now opening, at their old stand in Maysville, a large and elegant assortment of Merchandise, of the newest patterns, consisting in part of the following articles: (Long list of fabrics). A general assortment of medicines, hardware, Queens' ware, cutlery and groceries. From the liberal encouragement which we have heretofore, at all times, received we are induced to believe that our strict attention to business, as well as our regard for the interest of our customers, has received the approbation of the public; and we can therefore confidently solicit and continuance of patronage. We tender our sincere thanks to those who have supported us in our business, and hope still to retain our old, and obtain new customers, by selling goods as cheap as any persons west of the mountains. N.B. We particularly solicit country merchants to call and examine our goods as our stock is large. Maysville, Nov 8, 1826

The Maysville Eagle

New Goods, Henry Machir, has just received from New York, Philadelphia and Baltimore, and is now opening, at his store on Water Street, a large general and very superior assortment of Fall and Winter Goods. As these goods were purchased with cash at a most favorable moment, he can confidently say to the public, that those who desire good and substantial fabrics, and cheap bargains, for cash, will not be disappointed in giving him a call. Maysville, Nov. 1.

Philadelphia album and ladies literary gazette. Long article on the content. Address Thomas C. Clarke, Philadelphia.

Plank and Shingles. Thomas S. Starr, (At the foundry on Third Street) has on hand a quantity of assorted white pine plank, seasoned, fit for immediate use. Also, a quantity of White Pine shingles: which he offers for sale on such terms it will be no disadvantage to those about to make purchases, to give him a call. For further remarks, touching prices & c. be made. Maysville, 6th Sept. 1826

To Rent, the subscriber wishes to rent, for one or more years, the following described property, viz. One plantation, of about forty acres of cleared land on the Ohio and Big Sandy rivers, and including the ferry across said rivers, and tavern seat now occupied by Benjamin Maxey. Also, several small tenements, on the said river adjacent to the one above mentioned. Also A farm of 140? Acres of land, cleared in Adam County, Ohio, on the road from West ? to Chillicothe, one mile from the Steam Furnace, and including the tavern seat now occupied by Mr. Carrothers, formerly by James Allen. Also, one farm of 40 acres, cleared land, in Brown County, O. adjoining John Glendennin, two miles from Decator. Also, two small farms, lying in Clinton County, Ohio, one mile from Gillaspie's tavern, and near the road leading from Hillsborough to Urbana, now occupied by John Lyon. Also several small farms, on Li?? River in Fleming County Kentucky. Also 15 ¾ acres of cleared land adjoining the village of Mayslick, formerly occupied by William B. Williams. Also, two small farms in Nicholas County, Ky. five miles from the Lower Blue Licks, and two miles from the mouth of Johnson's fork, formerly occupied by Samuel Burden. I have also 15 or 20 small tracts of land, lying in different parts of the states of Ohio and Kentucky, which I would allow for good produce, such as horses, cattle, pork, castings, iron, wheat, hemp or tobacco. I have also four young stud horses all of which I would sell for cash or approved produce. One of them, a colt of two years old this spring, and sired by a whip horse, the property of Col. William Buford, For further particulars, apply to the subscriber, Daniel Morgan. Washington Ky. Feb. 28, 1827

The Maysville Eagle
Wednesday May 23, 1827

Historical from the Kentucky Gazette. Notes on Kentucky. Section XXVI. During these political struggles and difficulties, the Indians continued their depredations on the defenseless inhabitants of Kentucky. On the 11th April, in the year 1787, a party of 15 Indians attacked a family by the name of Shanks, on Cooper's run, Bourbon County. The family consisted of an old lady, her two sons from 18 to 22 years of age, a widow daughter with a small child in her arms, who occupied one end of a double cabin - while two single grown daughters, and a third about ten years of age, occupied the other end. A little after night a knocking at the door of the room occupied by the old lady was heard, and a call in good English "who keeps house." One of the family was about opening the door, when the old lady forbid it, saying they were Indians. The young men sprang for their guns and the enemy fled to the door of the three daughters, which opened on the side of the house, out of reach of the guns from the other part, the door of which opened at the end, in the passage formed by the cabins. The Indians finding the young women unprotected beat down the door with a rail, and attempted to take the three girls prisoners, one of whom they secured: the little girl broke out, and might have escaped by making off in the dark, but the poor thing ran around the house calling for help, and such was the feelings of the unhappy brothers, that they would have flew to her aid, if they had not been prevented by their aged mother, who forbid the door being opened, and in an instant the tomahawk of an Indian finished the cries of this little girl, in the hearing of her mother and brothers. While a party of the enemy were engaged in securing one of the other girls as a prisoner, and tomahawking the other, the third & eldest, defended herself with a knife used by her at her loom, where she was engaged at the moment of attack. The defense of this heroine deserved a better fate. She stabbed an Indian who fell dead at her feet: but she was overpowered and murdered.* Thus ended the conflict in one part of the house: of the three sister, two were killed and one made prisoner-- had the old lady permitted her two brave sons to take her off at this moment, the night was dark, and the dread of the enemy so great in approaching a rifle, the probability is, that all the other part of the family would have escaped. The Indians when in possession of the room occupied by the three sisters, set fire to it, and the flames extended to the other end, ...to a considerable distance. The Indians ported themselves in the dark in the angles of the yard fence, and waited for the flames to drive their prey from the house. The old lady, to infirm to run, placed herself under the protection of one of her sons, while the other took charge of his widowed sister, who had her infant in her arms. Under this arrangement they all left the house at the same time, and attempted to pass the yard fence at two different points. The old lady was shot dead in crossing the fence, and at the point where the others attempted to cross, several Indians rose upon them, one young man fell in gallantly defending his sister and her infant. Of those in the room containing 5 persons, two only fell, viz. The old lady and the youngest of the two brothers, while the rest escaped to the neighboring farms and alarmed the country. Early on the next day, Col. John Edwards, with about thirty men were on the spot, and witnessed a scene too shocking for description. Every thing was either destroyed or carried off. The Indian killed by the young lady with her weaving knife, was found in the hollow of a tree trunk in a branch near the house. While the massacre was going on and during the night, a snow fell much deeper than usual for the season. Col. Edwards, with the number of men above mentioned, started in the pursuit of the Indians, who were on foot, and made for the most hilly part of the country, formed by the waters of Eagle Creek on the left, and Licking river on the right. The trail of the Indians was so plain, that the men, who were all mounted, could push on as fast as the nature of the ground would permit, and late in the evening on the same day, found the young woman lying scalped and tomahawked, only a few minutes before - they having been notified of the pursuit by the cries of a dog, which had been permitted to follow the men from the house. A few friends were left to take charge of the expiring victim, while the rest of the party pursued on in full speed, and on the point of a narrow ridge, saw the Indians passing and repassing from one tree to another so quickly, that it was believed the whole party had prepared for battle. The men dismounted and approached cautiously from tree to tree, flanking to the right and left. The Indians continued one steady yell, to induce a belief of great strength. When the whites approached near enough, a fire commenced: one Indian was killed and another fled badly wounded. It appeared that these two were all that remained, who had no doubt agreed to sacrifice their lives for the safety of the rest of the party, by which means they gained so great a start as to enable them to reach a long branch, which was muddy by the melting of the snow, and night coming on, no farther traces of the savages could be found. Before the next morning the snow had disappeared, and the men returned home. From the blood on the blanket left by the wounded Indian, it was believed he could survive; and as he threw away his gun, he would not be able to make fire until he should meet with his party which could not take place that night.

In the summer of 1787, a person of savage appearance hailed house in Bourbon County, near the late residence of the unfortunate widow Shanks who had been killed the preceding spring. The person was answered from the house, and invited by signs as well as words, to come in - the invitation

The Maysville Eagle was accepted after a little hesitation, and the stranger, who appeared to be about 20 years of age, made the following narrative of himself in broken English, which he spoke very imperfectly. He stated that he was taken prisoner when too small to recollect his name, or the place from which he was taken, the rest of his family, he believed were killed. The Indians into whose, hands he fell, gave him to one of the party who had recently lost a son, and he was adopted instead of the lost child, and treated with all the tenderness of which his adopted parents were capable. He was instructed in the art of war and hunting, and partook of those pleasures near the Indian town on the waters of Lake Erie, where he resided until the present spring, when his adopted father took him and an only son, to hunt on the Miami River, about forty miles from where Cincinnati now stands. After a considerable quantity of meat was secured, the old man proposed to indulge his white and red sons, in a war trip to the settlements of Kentucky; where they both were anxious to display their skill in the art taught them by their warlike father. The prepared a bark canoe, and crossed the Ohio river a little below the mouth of Licking river, and secured their barque in some thick bushes on the Kentucky side, to prevent injury from the sun, which quickly destroys such frail water craft, if exposed. There remained some feelings of civil life in the bosom of this adopted son of the forest and as he approached the settlement and formed a plan of leaving his companions. He never thought of betraying them, never crossed his mind. The night before they reached the settlements, the old man heard an owl scream in the night, which he considered the forerunner of misfortune, he was about retracing his steps, when his white son remonstrated against it, and being joined by his red brother the fond father submitted to the entreaties of his children, and agreed to persevere in the previous plans of war. They went to sleep, and were soon roused by the old man, whose dreams had disturbed his sleep, which warned him of certain danger. The entreaties of the young men again prevailed over him, and he consented to continue the trip but would by no means agree to remain any longer in the place they then occupied, but removed some distance for the remainder of the night. The next day they reached the settlements, and at night were approaching a house, when this young man escaped in the dark, which frustrated all further attempts of the father and red son. All the signals agreed on to collect the party, were in vain. He remained concealed in the thick weeds until morning, when he hailed the house before stated. The neighborhood was alarmed, and the timid stranger was examined over and over again. Strong suspicions arose, that he was a spy employed by the enemy, and to remove all doubts, he was required to conduct his countrymen to the spot where the canoe had been concealed on the bank of the Ohio River. He remonstrated against this measure, and was greatly distressed at the idea of

The Maysville Eagle

assisting the death of his father and brother, whom he still loved. Nothing would satisfy the white men, short of some evidence to support his account of himself, and he was ultimately compelled to conduct a body of fifteen men in search of the canoe. He stated that on their way, his father had hid a kettle and some provisions fifteen miles on this side of the Ohio, to which place he would first conduct them - they were all mounted on good horses. Such had been the speed of the Indians that they were found seated by a fire cooking in the kettle when the whites arrived where it had been laid. At the request of the adopted son, an attempt was made to take them prisoners, but their exertions to get off were found to be such, that they were tired and the old man was mortally wounded, and did not expire until he had seen his distressed son who had betrayed him. The other Indian escaped unhurt, and the white men ordered their guide to conduct them to the canoe. In the deepest anguish he begged to be spared from another sight so distressing, as to be the cause of the death of his brother, the partner of al his former amusements- urging that he had now convinced them of the correctness of his first statement, and hoped they would require no further act so afflicting to his feelings - but they were not to be appeased, they mounted their guide again and continued the pursuit. It was fifteen miles to the canoe, and so precise was the skill of the son of the forest in finding his way to the spot, that he steered directly to it without the aid of the slightest trace of any sort. The men halted some little distance from the river bank, concealed their horses and then placed themselves in some thick bushes near the canoe. In about ten minutes the unfortunate Indian arrived and was about launching his canoe in the river, when he fell dead, pierced with several balls, and never experienced the pang which a sight of his treacherous brother must have produced. This adopted son of the forest was not required to assist in the killing of his father and brother. He suffered greatly and the writer of these notes has not been able to learn whether he still lives. If any additional information exists among the early settlers of this country, on this or any other subject, it would be thankfully received.

*There was no doubt that the Indian was killed by the young woman in the manner stated & the wound fitted the knife, and his death could be accounted for in no other way.

Judge Buel of Albany, on of the most scientific practical agriculturist in the United States has published the following remarks on the culture of potatoes...

A letter published in the Massachusetts Journal, gives a description of the ruins of a very ancient work of defense, situated in Gallatin County

The Maysville Eagle

Kentucky, a little below the confluence of the Ohio and Kentucky Rivers. They are on the summit of a hill which overlooks the courses of both those streams for ten or fifteen miles, and affords a level of about twenty acres. It is accessible from the Ohio valley only by a narrow ridge rising with a gradual ascent, which would be impassable in a carriage. It is separated from the neighboring highlands, by a deep valley and a stream, except in one place where a ridge connects them. The plain on the summit is surrounded by loose stones which have the appearance of an old wall completely ruined. There are estimated to be enough on the ground to build a wall five feet thick, and forty or fifty feet high. The stones have evidently been collected there with great industry, as loose stones are sparingly scattered over the neighboring land. A smooth space of twenty or thirty feet wide was dug out just within the wall, and still remains. In some places it passed through ledges of rock, where as well as on some stones in the ruins, there are evidently marks of the sledge. The two accessible points appear to have gates or entrances, defended by advanced mounds; and it is not improbable that a spring about two hundred feet bellow the walls might have been secured in some similar manner. The writer, however, supposes that the Ohio River once ran at a much greater elevation than at present, and might have passed near this fortification. The great antiquity of the work is proved by the fact that forest trees which grow upon the site, do not differ in any respect from those in the vicinity.

Mason Circuit - Sct. April Term, 1827. John Walton complainant, against Enoch Barr's heirs & others. It appearing to the satisfaction of the court that the defendant, Robert S. Barr, is not an inhabitant of this commonwealth, and he not having entered his appearance therein agreeable to the law and the rules of this court, upon motion of the complainant, it is ordered, that unless he appear here on or before the first day of the next term, and answer the complainant's bill, the same will be taken for confessed against him - and that a copy of this order be published in some authorized newspaper of Kentucky for two months successively. Marshall Key

Mason Circuit, Sct. April term 1827. Jacob Slack, complainant against William Barclay & others, def'ts. The defendants, William Barclay and Dorcus his wife, not having entered their appearance herein according to law an the rules of this court, and it appearing to the satisfaction of the court that they are not inhabitants of this commonwealth; upon motion of the complainant, it is ordered, that unless they appear here on or before the first day of the next term and answer the complainant's bill, the same will be taken for confessed against them, and that a copy of this order be

The Maysville Eagle
published in some authorized newspaper of Kentucky for two months successively. Marshall Key. Cl'k.

Mason Circuit, Sct. April Term 1827. Hannah Reed, complainant, against Henry Weirick, defendant. The defendant not having entered his appearance herein according to law and the rules of this court, and it appearing to the satisfaction of this court, that he is not an inhabitant of this commonwealth; upon motion of the complainant, it is ordered that unless he appear here on or before the first day of the next term, and answer the complainant's bill, the same will be taken for confessed against him - and that a copy of this order be published in some authorized newspaper in Kentucky for two months successively. Attest, Marshal Key, cl'k

Mason Circuit, Sct. April term 1827, John Armstrong, complainant against Henry Weirick, defendant The defendant not having entered his appearance herein according to law and the rules of this court, and it appearing to the satisfaction of this court, that he is not an inhabitant of this commonwealth; upon motion of the complainant, it is ordered that unless he appear here on or before the first day of the next term, and answer the complainant's bill, the same will be taken for confessed against him - and that a copy of this order be published in some authorized newspaper in Kentucky for two months successively. Attest, Marshal Key, Cl'k

Mason Circuit, Sct. April Term 1827. Lewis E. Reed, complainant, against Elijah Alexander & Oris Sterne The defendants not having entered his appearance herein according to law and the rules of this court, and it appearing to the satisfaction of this court, that he is not an inhabitant of this commonwealth; upon motion of the complainant, it is ordered that unless he appear here on or before the first day of the next term, and answer the complainant's bill, the same will be taken for confessed against him - and that a copy of this order be published in some authorized newspaper in Kentucky for two months successively. Attest, Marshal Key, cl'k

Mason Circuit, Sct. April Term 1827, Jabes (sic) Shotwell, complainant against John Shotwell's heirs, defendants. The defendants, John Wheeler and Eliza his wife; Edward Dobyns and Ann his wife, and Nathan Shotwell, not having entered their appearance herein according to law and the rules of this court, and it appearing to the satisfaction of this court, that they are not an inhabitant of this commonwealth; upon motion of the complainant, it is ordered that unless they appear here on or before the first day of the next

The Maysville Eagle

term, and answer the complainant's bill, the same will be taken for confessed against them - and that a copy of this order be published in some authorized newspaper in Kentucky for two months successively. Attest, Marshal Key, cl'k

Taken up by William Hendrickson, living on the waters of Cabin Creek, Poplar Flat, an iron grey filly, supposed to be two years old, a small star in the forehead; about 13 and a half hands high - appraised to $15 before me this nineteenth day of April, 1827. Thomas Parker, J.P.L.C. May 16

Mason Circuit, Sct. April Term 1827. Henry Weirick, complainant against George Weirick, defendant. The defendant not having entered his appearance herein according to law and the rules of this court, and it appearing to the satisfaction of this court, that he is not an inhabitant of this commonwealth; upon motion of the complainant, it is ordered that unless he appear here on or before the first day of the next term, and answer the complainant's bill, the same will be taken for confessed against him - and that a copy of this order be published in some authorized newspaper in Kentucky for two months successively. Attest, Marshal Key, cl'k

Mason Circuit, Sct. April Term 1827. James W. Moss complainant, against Daniel McKinney & others, def'ts. The defendant, William McKinney, The defendant not having entered his appearance herein according to law and the rules of this court, and it appearing to the satisfaction of this court, that he is not an inhabitant of this commonwealth; upon motion of the complainant, it is ordered that unless he appear here on or before the first day of the next term, and answer the complainant's bill, the same will be taken for confessed against him - and that a copy of this order be published in some authorized newspaper in Kentucky for two months successively. Attest, Marshal Key, cl'k

Mason Circuit, Sct. April Term 1827. Archibald Dixson, complainant against William H. Pepper and others, defts. The defendant, George Williams, not having entered his appearance herein according to law and the rules of this court, and it appearing to the satisfaction of this court, that he is not an inhabitant of this commonwealth; upon motion of the defendant, William H. Pepper, it is ordered that unless he appear here on or before the first day of the next term, and answer the cross bill, of the said William H. Pepper, the same will be taken for confessed against him - and that a copy of this order be published in some authorized newspaper in Kentucky for two months successively. Attest, Marshal Key, cl'k

The Maysville Eagle

Mason Circuit, Sct - April Term, 1827. Samuel Baldwin, complainant, against Edmund Collins & others, def'ts. The defendants, the unknown heirs of Richard Taylor, and Phillip Buckner, not having entered their appearance herein according to law and the rules of this court, and it appearing to the satisfaction of this court, that he is not an inhabitant of this commonwealth; upon motion of the defendant, it is ordered that unless they appear here on or before the first day of the next term, and answer the bill of the said defendant, Edmund Collins,, the same will be taken for confessed against them - and that a copy of this order be published in some authorized newspaper in Kentucky for two months successively. Attest, Marshal Key, cl'k

Mason Circuit, Sct. April Term, 1827. James Savage, complainant against Samuel Whipps and Jno. W. Anderson, defendants. The defendant, Samuel Whipps, not having entered his appearance herein according to law and the rules of this court, and it appearing to the satisfaction n of this court, that he is not an inhabitant of this commonwealth; upon motion of the complainant, it is ordered that unless he appear here on or before the first day of the next term, and answer the complainant's bill, the same will be taken for confessed against him - and that a copy of this order be published in some authorized newspaper in Kentucky for two months successively. Attest, Marshal Key, cl'k

Mason Circuit, Sct - April Term, 1827. Maurice Langhorne, complainant, against George H. Sinclair & others, defts. The defendant, George H. Sinclair, not having entered his appearance herein according to law and the rules of this court, and it appearing to the satisfaction of this court, that he is not an inhabitant of this commonwealth; upon motion of the complainant, it is ordered that unless he appear here on or before the first day of the next term, and answer the complainant's bill, the same will be taken for confessed against him - and that a copy of this order be published in some authorized newspaper in Kentucky for two months successively. Attest, Marshal Key, cl'k

Mason Circuit, Sct - April Term 1827. Benjamin Clift, complainant, against William Shelton's heirs, defendants. The defendants, Austin Shelton, Dabney Shelton, Thomas Shelton, John Shelton and Henry Shelton, not having entered their appearance herein according to law and the rules of this court, and it appearing to the satisfaction of this court, that they are not an inhabitant of this commonwealth; upon motion of the complainant, it is ordered that unless they appear here on or before the first

The Maysville Eagle
day of the next term, and answer the complainant's bill, the same will be taken for confessed against him - and that a copy of this order be published in some authorized newspaper in Kentucky for two months successively. Attest, Marshal Key, cl'k

Mason Circuit, Sct - April Term 1827. William Parker, complainant, against Lewis Bullock & others, defendants. The defendants, the unknown heirs of Charles Yancy, deceased, not having entered their appearance herein according to law and the rules of this court, and it appearing to the court that they are not inhabitants of this commonwealth; upon motion of the complainant, it is ordered that unless he appear here on or before the first day of the next term, and answer the complainant's bill, the same will be taken for confessed against him - and that a copy of this order be published in some authorized newspaper in Kentucky for two months successively. Attest, Marshal Key, cl'k

Wm. S. Bodley, Will practice law in the courts of Mason, Fleming and Lewis Counties. His office is in Maysville, on Front Street next door below Mr. John Roe's. Maysville, March 14, 1827

Maysville Eagle Wednesday May 23, 1827.

To the people of Mason County. Fellow Citizens: Having been announced a candidate to represent the county of Mason, in the next general assembly, you will, I feel confident, pardon me for presenting my views in relation to some leading points of policy, in which all classes of the community, and particularly the farming interest of the west, feel a deep and vital interest. Very long article which ends with. Fellow citizens, I have frankly presented you my views upon a subject, in which I, as a farmer, have a deep interest, in common with yourselves. I have never doubted as to the correctness of those views; and I entreat you to examine the subject calmly and deliberately, before you consent to put down an administration which is promoting your best interest, with a zeal and ability which cannot fail of success, provided they meet your support. Adam Beatty. 16th May, 1827.

Washington Inn. The subscriber has just opened a house of public entertainment in the town of Washington, at her old stand, the large brick home near the centre of Main Street, and where she recollects very gratefully the extensive custom then experienced. Determined by assiduously endeavoring to accommodate, agreeable, all travelers and others who may call, to merit a renewal of it, she solicits the attention of her friends, and a share of public favor. Her stable will be well supplied

The Maysville Eagle
and attended to. Jane Stith. Washington May 10. A few boarders would be agreeable.

August election. Candidates for Congress. Gen. Thomas Metcalfe, Administrar's.
Robert Scrogin, Esq. John Trimble, Esq., Rev. Dr. Leach, For Jackson. State Legislature. For the Administration: Adam Beatty, Esq. Francis T. Hord, Esq. Capt. James Byers: For Gen. Jackson: Mr. John Cowgill, William Worthington, Esq. Mr. James W. Bullock.
List of Candidates Continued. Fleming. William P. Fleming, (administration,) and Richard R. Lee, (Jacksonian,) for the senate. Joseph Secrest and Thomas Jackson (Jacksonians,) for the House of Representatives.
Barren. William B. Cook (adm'r) and R. D. Maupin (Jack) for the senate. Col. Asa Young, General Franklin ... W. Hall, (all adm'r) for the ..Representatives; James G. Hardy, ...
Nelson. Benjamin ... Samuel T. Beall, for the senate ... and Jonathan Simpson, for the house of representatives. (Ink blot on paper, can not read all of the names.)

Colonization Society. The annual meeting of the "Maysville Auxiliary Colonization Society," was held in the Presbyterian Meeting house on Wednesday last. An address, appropriate to the occasion, was delivered by John Chambers, Esq. of Washington. The following gentlemen were elected officers of the Society for the ensuring year. Rev. John T. Edgar, President. Adam Beatty, Esq. 1st Vice President, James Morris, Esq. 2nd Vice President, John Chambers, Esq. Corres. Secretary, William Huston, Jr. Rec. Secretary, Andrew M. January, Treasurer. Managers. Francis Taylor, Esq. Maj. Val. Peers, Capt. Thomas Nicholsen, Rev. Walter Warder, Jas. M. Runyon, Johnston Armstrong, Peter Grant, Isaac Qutten and Lewis Collins.

The Rev. Dr. Leach, of Nicholas County, is said to be a candidate for Congress from this district, and in favor of Gen. Jackson for the presidency. We would advise the Reverend Doctor, in the most friendly manner, to attend to his flock and his patients. It ill becomes him who has sent himself up as "a preacher of righteousness" and a pattern of "divine morality," to engage in a political warfare which is calculated to bring into active exercise the worst passions of our nature; It should rather be his province, we think, from the sanctity of his profession, to proclaim "peace and good will among men." Whether our advice is received in the spirit it is given, is probably, not very important. One thing, however, is evident - General

The Maysville Eagle

Jackson carries weights in this district, under which a much more formidable popularity could not sustain itself. As it is the general wish that there should be a fair test of the strength of the administration and of Jackson, we hope the friends of the general will withdraw at least two of their candidates from the field of competition in this district.

The late robbery. On Wednesday morning the 9th inst. Wm. H. Rice was taken into custody near Norton, and Delaware County, by Col. Brotherton and Mr. John Kelly of this town, whilst proceeding in a hack to Portland. On examining his person about $30 in specie was found. Search was for some time made for the residue of the money, and the sum mentioned in our last was found rolled up in a shirt in the bottom of the back. While they were examining the cash he made his escape into the woods, but with some difficulty was again taken. He was brought before a justice of the peace on his arrival in Columbus, and committed to prison. He stated upon oath, that two black men of this town proposed to him the plot-made him take an oath not to disclose, and were the accomplices who carried it into execution. The two Negroes were arrested, their houses searched, but nothing found. There being no other evidence against them they were discharged, and it seems to be the general opinion that they are innocent. As he has implicated different individuals, not much reliance perhaps can be placed upon his statements. Rice has resided in this place since some time in December. His native place we believe is Baltimore. The money has all been recovered, except about one thousand and fifty dollars. The two persons mentioned in the last, are suspected of being accomplices, have been honorably acquitted. Ohio State Jour.

Deaths. In Mayslick, Mason County, KY on Tuesday morning last, after a long and severe illness, which she bore with Christian fortitude and resignation, Mrs. Jane Mackey, consort of Mr. William Mackey, late a merchant of that place and daughter of Gen. Robert Pague of Mason County.

Literary Notice. John T. Edgar has the pleasure to inform the patrons of his Academy, and the public in general, that he has obtained the consent of Mrs. Rector, formerly of Lexington, Ky. To take the charge of his Female Department. Mrs. Rector will enter upon the duties of a Tutoress immediately; and for her character and literary qualifications, persons are hereby referred to Samuel January, Esq. of Limestone, A.M. January of this place; and Dr. Blythe and other scientific gentlemen of Lexington.

The Maysville Eagle

Confectionery. The subscriber respectfully informs the public in general, and his friends in particular, that he has opened a Confectionery establishment at the sign of Napoleon Buonaparte, Upper Market, Cincinnati, where he will be prepared to accommodate those who may favor him with their custom, with every article usually looked for in his line of business. Young gentlemen can be accommodated with board by the day, week, or any longer period. He ventures to hope that his experience in keeping an establishment of the kind proposed, and the exertions he is determined to make use of, to do justice to those who may give him a call, will be rewarded by a generous share of public patronage. Jno. W. Kothe (Rothe?) Cincinnati May 17, 1826.

Dancing School. E. H. Bull, respectably informs the Ladies and Gentlemen of Maysville, that he will open his school at Capt. Langhorne's Room on Friday, the 25th inst. At 10 o'clock, a.m. and continue every Friday and Saturday until the close of he session. For terms &c. Inquire at Capt. Langhorne's Bar. May 28, 1827.

Administrator's Sale. Will be offered at Public Sale, at the late residence of Jacob Boone deceased, in the town of Maysville, on the first Saturday in June, the personal property belonging to the estate of the said deceased, consisting of household & kitchen furniture, one horse, cow & c. Nine months' credit will be given on all sums over five dollars, the purchaser giving bond and approved security. Sale to commence at 10 o'clock a.m. William Boone, Adm'r. N.B. All persons indebted to said estate, either by note or book account, are requested to make immediate payment; and those having claims, will present them, without delay, properly authenticated for adjustment. W.B.

Apprentices to the blacksmith business. Two Youths, of industrious habits, and of good moral character, will be taken as apprentices to the blacksmith business. Apply to Absalom White. Mayslick, Mason Co. Ky.

Light infantry orders. The Maysville Light Infantry Company will parade on Friday the 8th of June next, at 8 o'clock, a.m. at the market house, in the town of Maysville, completely armed and equipped - and from thence to march to the jail of this county, there to act as a guard while the sheriff is executing a Negro man, Harry, a slave, who is to be hanged on that day. Stephen Lee, Capt. May 23,

The Maysville Eagle

Troop Orders. The Washington Troop are notified to meet at Washington, on the above mentioned day at 10 o'clock, for the purpose therein specified. Thos. Nicholson, Capt. May 23.

Masonic. Mayslick Lodge. No. 74, will celebrate the approaching anniversary of St. John the Baptist, on Saturday, the 23rd of June next, by a public procession. Neighboring lodges and transient brethren are respectfully invited to join us on that occasion. It is expected that a sermon will be preached. Berry Dobyns. Chairman of the Committee. Mayslick, May 23.

Eagle Tavern, Washington, Kentucky Removal. Joseph H. Hudnut. Respectfully informs his friends and the public, that he has taken the large brick building on Main Street, Washington, (heretofore occupied by Mr. James Artus) where he is prepared to accommodate travelers and others who may favor him with their custom, in a manner which he trust, cannot fail to render general satisfaction. Pledging himself to use every exertion to promote the comfort of his customers, he respectfully solicits a portion of public patronage. Washington, May 16, 1827.

The thorough bred and distinguished running horse, Paragon, is standing for the present season in Washington, Mason County, Ky. Persons desirous of putting mares to this fine, blooded, beautiful and distinguished race horse, will have the strictest attention given by calling. John W. Anderson. May 9. This continues with a long column on Paragon's lineage. We deem it unnecessary to say more of Paragon, as he is well known in Kentucky as a Race Horse, and we ask the question, is it possible that a horse of his blood, performance, beauty & c. can fail to produce fine stock, either for the turf, saddle or harness? J.S.Berryman, R.G. Jackson.

The celebrated race horse, Doublehead, is in fine health & spirits and consequently well qualified to serve those who call on him at Washington. Knowsley is progressing at Germantown and Mr. Burgess's near Minerva. After an examination of our bills, we have only to request those who wish to raise fine horses, to call and examine our horses before they make their engagements. James H. Holton, Edmund Thornton

Kentucky, Lewis Circuit Court, Sct. March Term 1827. John Tilford & others, compl'ts against Robert Grant & others, def'ts. This day came the complainants, by their attorney, and it appearing to the satisfaction of the court, that the defendant, George W. Clendenen, is not an inhabitant of this commonwealth, and having failed to enter his appearance herein, agreeably to law and the rules of this court, it is ordered, that unless the said defendant, George W. Clendenen, do appear here on or before the first day of the next term of this court, and file his answer, plea or demurer, to the complainants' bills, that the same will be taken us confessed, as to him - and that a copy of this order be inserted in some authorized newspaper of this state for two months successively, according to law. And the cause is continued until the next term of this court. A copy Teste, Joseph Robb, C.L.C.C.

Greenup Circuit & County - Sct. April Term of the Greenup Circuit Court, 1827. Edmund Phillips, complainant, against Daniel Durbin, defendant, This day came the defendant herein, but complainant in a cross bill filed in this cause by the said Daniel Durbin against John Kenton and George Mason, by his counsel, and the defendant in said cross bill, George Mason, not having entered his appearance to said cross bill, agreeable to law and the rules of this court, and it appearing to the satisfaction of the court that the said George Mason is not an inhabitant of this commonwealth; it is, on motion of the said Daniel Durbin, ordered by the court, that the said George Mason enter his appearance herein on or before the first day for the next term of this court, and answer the cross bill of the said Daniel Durbin, filed in this cause; or that on failure thereof, the same will be taken for confessed against him - and it is further ordered, that a copy of this order be forthwith published in some authorized newspaper of this state for two calendar months in succession. Test, John Hockaday, C.G.C.C.

A bargain in land. On the Saturday before the second Monday in June, about 212 acres of land, in Mason County, now occupied by Mr. Hamilton and Mr. Campbell, adjoining the residence of the late Capt. Henry Graham, will be offered at public sale, to the highest bidder, on the premises. But if not sold so as to render the heirs of Robert Douthet safe, in the sum advanced for it, it will not be struck off, but again offered at the court house door in Washington, on the second Monday in June next. And in the mean time, Robert Douthet, one of the heirs, expects to be in the county himself, and may be consulted for particulars, on private bargain. A general warranty deed will be made. The title is good beyond a doubt. Walker Reid, Attorney. April 11, 1827

Horse-Wheel for sale. I wish to sell the horse wheel and drum which have been attached to my Cotton Factory. The cog wheel is eighteen feet in diameter, the horse walk twenty-eight; and from the proportion, it has run the lightest, and with the least power of any wheel I ever saw. I will sell it very low. Val. Peers. Maysville, 6th March 1827.

The Maysville Eagle

January & Huston, have just received, at their commission house, with the following articles. Long list including buffalo robes, bourbon, Monongahela whiskey, and teas. All of which they will sell low for cash or barter for feathers, hemp, leaf tobacco, Ginseng, beeswax, rages & c. Maysville, March 21, 1826

Real Estate for sale. The undersigned, as Executor of the estate of the late Alexander Dougherty of Mason County, deceased, offers for sale the following described Real Estate. The home farm, being the late residence of the said decedent, lying within two miles of Mayslick, and containing 500 acres of first rate land, well adapted for a stock farm, with 300 or more acres cleared, and under good fence - a large brick dwelling, brick stable and barn, smoke house and kitchen - and a tan yard, with all the necessary buildings for tanning with 24 or 25 vats. A house and lot in Mayslick formerly occupied by William Mackey as a store, and now occupied by Capt. Thomas Rudd. Tavern Stand, a house and lot, in the same place, occupied by Elias Tapp as a tavern - which has a back lot and a large stable attached to it. Also, A quantity of oak land, laying on the waters of Shannon, which will be sold in quantities to suit purchasers. Persons wishing to purchase any of the above described property, will please call upon the subscriber, at the farm first above mentioned. Payments to be made in such installments as shall be agreed upon the parties. Thos. M. Dougherty, Ex'r. Mason County, May 2,

100 Dollars Reward. Lost, on Friday evening last, in Maysville, or between my house and Maysville, a small red morocco pocket book, tied with a green ribbon. It contained seven hundred and twenty dollars in United States' paper - two post notes of one hundred dollars each - several bills of $50 each, and some twenty dollar bills. No other papers or money recollected. Garrison Baldwin. May 9

Wool Carding. The subscriber having purchased the carding machines of Jacob Drake, is now ready to receive wool, and from his strict attention to business, with a first rate carder and new cards, flatters himself to be able to give general satisfaction to all who may please to favor him with their custom. The highest price will be given for flax seed, wool and such other articles of country produce as may be approved of. Wilson Clift. Mayslick, May 9

Wool Carding and spinning. The undersigned begs leave to inform the public that, having purchased the wool factory, formerly occupied by Mr.

The Maysville Eagle

William Richey, in the town of Washington, has with great care and attention, put the Machinery in a complete state of repair, and having procured the best quality of Eastern Cards, and of a suitable site to card the finest wool, together with the skill of his carder and spinner, and his own experience and entire attention to the factory, he feels confident that his work will be …….. shall be used to dispatch work in the shortest notice; and in so case shall his employers be compelled to call the second time for their work, if in his power to avoid it. His price for carding is $1-4 cents per pound. The wool must be well washed, and clean of burrs, or an additional charge will be made for washing and picking. He will spin wool for 10 cents per dozen any size under 16 cuts out of the pound; for any size over 16 cuts, he will spin for 12 1-2 cents per dozen. Janes, carpeting & flannels, will be manufactured on the shares, or otherwise on advantageous terms, and in superior manner. Good clean wool, and many other articles of country produce will be taken in payment. Enos Woodward. Washington May 5.

The well bred horse Plenipo. Long article. It concludes with Pedigree. Plenipo's sire was the noted horse old Plenipo that belonged to Mr. John Culbertson of Clark County Kentucky. His pedigree is equal to any horse in America, but too long for an advertisement; suffice it to say that he was got by the imported horse M…ger, and his dam raised by Mr. Rideout… of Annapolis in the state of Maryland.. will appear by the annex certificates of .. dam was formerly the property of Isaac Trumbo of Bourbon county, and was so fine a mare that she took the silver cup at the Lexington Agricultural show. he was got by the noted horse Welldigger, and he by the imported horse Speculator. Plenipo can beat any stud horse of his age in the state, a three mile heat. William Wells. Attest - Andrew Trumbo, Isaac Trumbo March 9th 1827. The following is a certificate to establish the blood of the old horse. I do certify, that the horse called Plenipo, a beautiful bay, with black mane and tail, ten years old last spring, is a full bred horse, got by the imported horse Messenger, and came out of the full bred mare Fatima. She was raised by John Rideout, Esq. Near Annapolis, in Maryland. The said horse Plenipo I have this day sold to Mr. John Culbertson of Clark County, Ky. I do hereby warrant the said horse to be as well bred as any horse in America. Witness my hand and seal this 26th day of September, 1803. Tobias Rudolph, seal. Attest - Thomas C. Clark. I hereby certify that the above Tobias Rudolph, Esq. Is one of the officiate Justices of the county aforesaid, and that due faith and credit is to be given to his certificate as well in courts of justice as thereout. In testimony whereof I have set my hand, and affixed the seal of my office, this 26th of Sept. 1803. John Baxter, Clerk Cecil County Court. Young Plenipo's character as a great

The Maysville Eagle

foal getter. We the undersigned being well acquainted with the stud Plenipo for the last two or three years, and having a knowledge of many of his colts, certify, that we believe him to be the best foal getter that has stood in Bath county within our recollection. He is now the property of Wm. Wells, of Fleming County, Ky. Give under our hand this 28th day of December 1822
John Crocket, William Atkinson, Jacob Trumbo, Isaac Coniers, Andrew Trumbo, David Utery, Alex. McIntire, William Baly, Warren Baley, Washington Iles, Andrew Cartmill, Jeremiah Corbin, Samuel Hodge.

For Sale, A Negro Woman, I offer my Negro Woman for sale. She is an elegant spinner, a good nurse, and an excellent house keeper. For particulars, apply to Nicholas Young, Baker, Maysville, April 25.

Removal. Take notice - all those indebted to the subscriber, are requested to call on him in the town of Washington, at the house formerly occupied by G. Adams & Co. and settle their respective accounts by the first day of June next; after which time all his unsettled demands will be put into the hands of an officer for collection. As he has abandoned his former occupation, it is peculiarly important to him that his business should be promptly and speedily a... James Artus. Washington May 16, 1827.

We wish to barter salt, for 300,000 lbs. Bacon. For which we will give the highest market price. 2,000 yds. Flax linen. 3,000 yds. Tow linen. We will give salt at 50 cents per bushel, the purchaser always paying the inspection here, as we are compelled to pay the inspection at Kenhawa. Johnston Armstrong, Peter Grant. Maysville.

M'Cormick Ploughs. J & L. Jacobs. Respectfully inform the farmers of Mason, Bracken, Lewis, Fleming, Nicholas, & c. in Kentucky and Clermont, Adam, Brown, Highland &c. in Ohio, that they have commenced, and will continue the manufacture, in the town of Maysville, of the above named highly finished and unrivaled Ploughs. They will be made of various sizes, (with corresponding prices) from the heavy two horse, to a size which will be drawn with ease by one horse. This celebrated plough has never failed, at all the agricultural fairs at which it has been exhibited, to take the premium awarded for the best plough. The following certificate, from a gentleman who witnessed its performance at Washington, in Mason county, on Monday last, are submitted to the public with the confident assurance that the opinions of these gentlemen will receive that weight which their general knowledge of agricultural implements entitle them. Gentlemen who wish to purchase the above ploughs, will find a quantity of all sizes, at all times on hand, at our manufactory on Third street, a short distance above Mr. Boon's new brick steam mill. Maysville, April 11, 1827. Certificate. We the undersigned subscribers, having witnessed the performance, this day, of one of the Messrs. Jacobs' Ploughs, known as the "M'Cormack Plough," give it as our decided opinion, that we have never before seen a Plough so admirably calculated to answer the object of its formation - being of easy draft, managed without difficulty, and uniformly and regularly inverting the whole award or slice of earth which it cuts. Rice Boulton, Whitfield Craig, Robert Walton, April 9, 1827.

J. Hanson, of the late firm of Davis & Hanson, having been re-appointed as auctioneer for this city, has taken that commodious Brick Warehouse, corner of Third and Wood streets, opposite R. Stewart's Pittsburgh Hotel, where he will transact auction and commission business, generally, and make liberal advances on consignments when acquired. Orders for goods, accompanied by cash, acceptances, or approved references, will be punctually attended to. Goods received on Storage, or forwarded at reasonable rates. Public sales of dry goods, &c. Every Thursday at 10 o'clock am. Pittsburgh, April 1827.

Greenup Circuit & County - Sct. April term of Greenup Circuit Court, 1827. Jonathan Morton's heirs and John Lawson complainants, against John Haweis' h'rs & others, d'fts. This day came the complainants, by their counsel, and the defendants, Edward Wilson, Thomas Wilson, and George Wilson, children of Mary Wilson, dec'd. William Bailes and John Bailes, children of Frances Bailes, dec'd. who was one of the children of Mary Wilson, dec'd., not having entered their appearance herein, agreeable to law and the rules of this court, and it appearing to the satisfaction of the court that they are not inhabitants of this commonwealth: Therefore, on motion of the said complainant, it is ordered that the said defendants do appear here on the first day of the next term of this court, and answer the complainant bill, or, that on failure thereof, the same will be taken for confessed against them - and it is further ordered, that a copy of this order be inserted in some authorized newspaper of this state for two calendar months in succession. A copy, Teste, John Hockaday, C.G.C.C.

Six Cents Reward. Ran away from the subscriber, on the 23rd of March, an indented apprentice to the boot and shoemaking business, named James Milbourn. He is 18 years of age, upwards of six feet high, pretty well made - had on when he went away, a suit of gray janes, and took with him other clothing not recollected The above reward but no charges, will be paid to

The Maysville Eagle
any person delivering said youth to me in Maysville. A.P. Stewart. April 11, 1827.

Maysville, Ky. Wednesday, July 11, 1827.

White Washing. Leonard, otherwise called Leonard Meads, (a colored man) respectfully makes known to the citizens of Maysville, that he is prepared to White Wash rooms, with very white lime, on the shortest notice and most reasonable terms. Persons wanting white washing done, can find him at Mr. John Sumrall's

Domestic Wine. We are glad to find, by the following paragraph from the Norfolk Herald, that our own opinion of Maj. Adlum's Wine is supported by that of others so respectable. "We have examined several samples of wine made by Major Adlum, from his vineyard, in the District of Columbia, which, for richness and flavor, are not surpassed by similar kinds of wine of European vintage. This is another evidence of the peculiar facility of our country of being blessed, with a solid and climate genial to the production of whatever can be supplied from almost every part of the globe, and of our independence, naturally as well as politically, of the old world. Of the perfection of which Major Adlum has brought the culture of the grape, and the delicacy and richness of his wines, we have often heard, and it has been a matter of surprise to us, that others, with perhaps greater advantages (in North Caroline for example) have not followed his example.

Col. Bodens, who was very fat, being accosted by a man to whom he owed money, with a how-do-ye-do? "Pretty well, thank you; you find I hold my own." "Yes, (rejoined the other) and mine too, to my sorrow."

A letter from Andrew Jackson to Mr. Carter Beverley. Of a political nature. The subscribers, citizens of Wheeling, do hereby certify that the above and foregoing, purporting to be a letter from Andrew Jackson to Carter Beverley is a true copy of a letter handed by the aid Carter Beverley on this day to Noah Zane, Esq. In Wheeling, as the original letter from Gen. Andrew Jackson to him the said Carter Beverley, which was received by mail last evening and post marked Nashville, June 9. Noah Zane, Moses M. Chaplin, Morgan Nelson, Wm.S. Peterson Full political page

The oration of Mr. Benjamin F. Reeve, delivered at Hieatt's on the 4th inst. Shall appear in the Eagle next week. .

The Maysville Eagle

Slave holders. We are requested to inform the slave holders of Mason County, that a meeting of that description of persons will be held at the courthouse in Washington, on Saturday, the 21st of July, inst. For the purpose of concerning measures for the better security of their property.

Judge Rochester, the secretary of the mission to the South American congress, arrived in this county about two weeks since from New Orleans, on a visit to his relative, Judge Beatty. He still, we believe, remains in Kentucky.

Two slight shocks of an Earthquake were experienced in this place on Thursday morning last, about 6 o'clock.

Fourth of July 1827. In pursuance to previous arrangements, a number of ladies and gentlemen repaired on Wednesday the 4th of July, to a most delightful spot of woodland, owned by Mr. William Gates, to celebrate the 51st anniversary of American Independence. The day, after the morning, was fine, and although the company was pretty large, unusual good order prevailed thro' out the day. After partaking of a sumptuous repast prepared for the occasion the company was addressed by Benjamin F. Reeve, on the subject of our independence &c. The Declaration of Independence was also read, after which Major Benjamin P. Thomas was appointed President, Capt. Benjamin Norris Vice President, Capt. Benjamin Reeve Secretary. The following toast were drank. ..... Volunteers. By Leander Hart. The patriots of America - May they follow the precepts laid down by the immortal Washington. By Ira Anderson. Damnation to all those who object is private aggrandisement at the expense of the community. By Capt. Benj. Norris. Gen. Thomas Metcalfe, our representative in Congress - His good sense, tried republicanism, and undeviating firmness, merits the apprebation and support of every friend to his country. By Amos Sroufe, Gen. Z.M.Pike, he bled and died in our cause, though in the height of victory. By Joshua Winters. The Militia of the U.S. the strength and honor of the nation - May their attention be unremitting in the acquirement of military knowledge. By John Davis. The people of the west - May they unite in harmony, lay aside their party divisions, and be enabled to counteract the combined coalition now in exercise against them. By Benj. F. Reeve. The combined coalition of the freemen of the United States - May they be ever enabled to defeat and put down any tyrant that may hope to rule over them. By Thos. H. Fox. General Washington - First in war, first in peace, and first in the hearts of his countrymen. By George S. Calvert. Gen. Andrew Jackson, the hero of New Orleans - May the eminent services that he rendered his country be promulgated and applauded by the

The Maysville Eagle

free born sons of Columbia. By John L. Thompson. The American fishermen - Success to them all, except such as fish for office. By Wm. Gates, Sen., Our military chieftains - they fought for our liberty and gained it, and we will maintain. Washington our first president, Jackson our next. By Wm. Gates, jr. Of all the soil that's in the west, Kentucky Clay I like the best. By Wm. Dunn, of Norfolk, Va. May the hinges of friendship between the citizens of Virginia and Kentucky near want greasing.

At a celebration of the Anniversary of American Independence at Mr. S. Hieatt's near Minerva, Col. John Mannen was called to the chair, and Mr. B. H. Rankins appointed vice president, Mr. A. Soward secretary - when after the removal of the cloth, the following toasts were drank. Volunteers. By W.B. Durrett. Lafayette - The patriot and philanthropist: His life, like the rainbow, presents an arch of heavenly beauty. By M. M'Closkey. Gen. Warren - the first American general who fell in the cause of our independence. By. Dr. A. H. Peck. "Fill to the brave who contend in the field, and the heroes who strive on the ocean, Tis duty that moves us the tribute to yield, and gratitude seconds the motion." By A. Beatty, Esq. Henry Clay - the eloquent friend of human liberty throughout the world, and the able advocate of the internal improvements and domestic manufactures. By J.W. Bullock. Gen. Andrew Jackson - Once the choice of the people; May they yet remain firm in his support. By S.W. Craig. The present Administration: May we always have such. Dr. A.J. Peck, Military Chieftains. Washington our first; Jackson our next President. By J.W. Bullock. The right of instruction. The guardian of our interest and spirit of our government. May those who disregard it, be disregarded by their constituents. By J. Best, Gen. A. Jackson, Though much abused by his enemies, may he triumph over all opposition, and fill the Presidential chair with honor and glory to his county. By Dr. W.B. Johnston. John Quincy Adams and Henry Clay: Two of Nature's nobility - unrivaled in talents - famed for integrity - admired by the liberal = beloved by the good - Cease! Ye calumniators! Your shafts fall harmless at their feet. By W.P. Thomas, May he who mounts a hobby to ride into office, be thrown into the mudhole of contempt. By M.M'Closkey. The Genius of Clinton: Our canals will ever be monuments to his memory. By A. Soward. Gen. Thos. Metcalfe, our distinguished Representative in Congress: May he receive that support to which his eminent services entitle him. (When this toast was drank, the general arose, and in a very short and feeling manner, expressed his thanks for the friendly manner in which he had been noticed.) By Col. J. Mannen - Our distinguished guest Col. Conn - May he receive that liberal support to which his principles entitle him. By W.B. Durrett. "Let the South boast its mountains of gold - Let the East boast its rubies

The Maysville Eagle

and pearls - but we boast a happier land, where mind is enlightened and free, and where woman is the pride and solace of Man."

Communicated. The Fourth of July was celebrated at the Sinking Spring, on Mill Creek. A barbecue was prepared by a number of the neighbors, and very generally attended, the company amounting to between 4 and 500 persons. The day was fine and pleasant, after dinner, when the cloth was removed the company assembled around the table, when Col. Duval Payne was appointed President, Mr. Septimus D. Clark Vice President, and Thomas Y Payne secretary, when the following toast prepared for the occasion were drunk with great cheering and apparent unanimity - after which several volunteer toasts were drunk, and the company separated in perfect order, harmony and peace. Volunteer Toast. By the President of the day. "Principles, not men." By the Vice president. "The President of the day." By the Secretary. Let Americans, with grateful plaudity, hail the fair name of the Maj. Gen. Brown, not second to any military chieftain. By Capt. James Byers. The Secretary of State - that page of history which hands to posterity the name of Henry Clay, will be among the brightest, proudest, in American annals. By Jesse Summers. American Independence _ May it never be shaken by a strange political union or combination. By E.B. Barker. The North, the South, the East , the West, General Jackson is the best. By Mr. Thomas W. Nelson. Internal improvements - The constitution delegates the power to congress; may they exert it in such a manner as to bind in chains indissoluble our free and happy union. By Jefferson Evens. The present administration - Guided by political wisdom, and enforced with moral integrity, must triumph over an unhallowed opposition. By E.B. Hannegan, Jackson - The friend of internal improvements, independent of any sinister motives; be hard and preserver of our rights and liberty .. Second struggle against the enemies of all free governments, the British tyrant. By J. Burgess. Henry Clay - The brightest star in the American constellation; though base falsehood and distraction has endeavors to rob him of an honest and imperishable fame - Yet his country, when he shall retire from the political world, will say, "well done thou good and faithful servant." By Sam. McAdow, the 4th July '76 - Gave birth to a nation of freemen and their sons are determined to preserve the inestimable inheritance while an arm remains to shield, or a heart to bleed in its defense.

We learn from the Philadelphia Aurora, that in the course of a few weeks about one hundred and twenty - five miles of canal will be placed under contract by the Pennsylvania Canal Commissioners, including one section on the Susquehanna, one on the Juniata, one on the Kisskimimtas, and

The Maysville Eagle

another on French Creek. Arrangements have also been made for an early commencement of the Delaware line, if the estimate shall fall within the limit of expense fixed by the Legislature. In addition to the regular engineers, several engineers have been temporarily employed to execute the surveys pointed out by law. Of this number two have already commenced operations, namely Major John Wilson, on the route through Chester and Lancaster counties, and Mr. John Randel, jr. On the north Branch of the Susquehanna. Two parties, under the direction of William Wilson, and Mr. John Mitchell, have been dispatched to take further examinations as to the practicability of a water communication between the Allegheny and Susquehanna Rivers.

Dr. William Adams, of Schenectady, aged 97 years lately arrived in Litchfield, Conn. Having performed the distance of upwards of 70 miles a day. The day following his arrival he was seen moving about Litchfield with ease and agility. The object of his visit is to spend the summer with a granddaughter. He has been a practicing physician in Schenectady upwards of 70 years.

A few days since, while Mr. Burgess of Fairfield, was engaged in manufacturing potash, and in the act of drying a batch of salts, a part of it began to melt, the kettle being covered for the purpose. In a short time he observed an unusual appearance in the form of one of them, upon which he stepped back, and in a moment it exploded with a loud noise and threw the burning salt in every direction. The report was heard a mile away, and was supposed to be that of a cannon. Mr. Burgess and a young man, who was present at the time received no bodily injury although their clothes were nearly destroyed

Wheat Wanted. I wish to purchase a few thousand bushels of wheat, to be delivered immediately after harvest, for which I will pay either ash or salt. Isaac Lewis. Mason County, July 11

The celebrated race horse, Paragon, has commenced his fall season at my stable, two miles East of Germantown, Mason County, and will be let to mares at ten dollars, payable by the 25th March, 1827. Mares which were put to Paragon during the spring season, and have not proved with foal, shall have the fall season without pay. Pasturage for mares from a distance will be furnished gratis; and all possible care taken to prevent accidents, but I will not be responsible for any that may happen. John W. Anderson. Mason County, Ky. July 11. Bellaire will stand for a fall season at the stable of Garrison Baldwin, near Maysville.

The Maysville Eagle

Notice, to the 15th Regiment K.M. Those persons belonging to said regiment, who were fined at the last court of assessment, are informed that they can have an opportunity of being heard on the first Monday of August, being the first day of the election. John Mannen, Col. 15th R.K.M. July 11.

Partial article, the first part is unreadable. Mr. Poyntz knows, or ought to know, that when he was about to purchase the flour, (in which he says he was defrauded) that I told him the wheat of which it was made was not good, and I did not think it would suit the Maysville market; but he might probably sell it on the way down the river. His reply was, (after examining the flour,) that "it was good enough." The accusation of fraud on my part, is erroneous and unjust, and demands reparation. R. L. Waters.

Lost, A red Morocco Pocket Book. Somewhere between Maysville & Mayslick on Friday the 6th instant. It has my name written in the inside; and had in it $10 U.S. paper, a bill of sale from Charles T. Marshall for a Negro man, and various other papers which I do not now recollect, which may be of importance to me, and of no use to any one else. I will give five dollars for the Pocket book, money and papers delivered to me, or to Sumrall & Adams of Maysville, or Joshua Linthicum of Mayslick Thomas Clarke. Mason County, July 11.

$50 Reward. Ran away from the subscriber, on the 9th of the present month. A Negro Man, named Reuben, very black about 32 years of age, five feet 11 inches high, bald on the top of his head, he is a cunning, artful fellow. I have no doubt he is making for Canada. He has a variety of clothing, with a new fur hat. The above reward will be paid, if taken out of this state; $20 if taken in the state; or $10 if taken in the county - and secured in jail or brought home to me, living near Mayslick, Mason County, Ky. Leroy Dobyns.

Hercules aided by Iolas destroying the Hydra. Potter's Vegetable Catholicon. The proprietor of this invaluable medicine, feels authorized, by its increasing reputation, to recommend it as superior to all other popular remedies, for the cure of King's Evil or Scrofula - Necrosts or diseased bones - Syphilis in every stage - Mercurial disease - Rheumatism - Liver complaints - and Ulcers of every description - The Catholicon has also been used with great success in every variety of Cutaneous disease, blotches on the face, pimples & tetter in particular: White Swellings, gout, jaundice and bilious diseases generally, dyspepsia or Indigestion, complaints of the stomach and general debility. It is a certain purifier of

The Maysville Eagle

the blood and humours and has been found an efficacious remedy in purifying the blood of children after vaccination, and should be invariably used as a general alternative both for children and adults - being agreeable to the most delicate palate, and a grateful cordial to the stomach. This is the first discovery f a medicine taken into the stomach, that has had the long desired effect of curing the most obstinate and distressing external diseases. The use of nutritious food, and the ordinary avocations of business, are not interrupted by the Catholicon; and its properties having the power of restoring both flesh and bone, and of renovating and invigorating every part of the system during the process of exterminating disease, is without parallel. For sale at the drug store of Dr. William R. Wood. Agent, Maysville, Ky. Certificates Philadelphia, Feb. 20, 1827. Mr. Wm. W. Potter: Dear Sir- Ten months have now elapsed since my daughter Mary Ann has been, by the use of your invaluable medicine, restored to a date of much better health than we could reasonably have expected and as a duty I owe to suffering humanity, and gratitude to yourself, I tender this, trusting it may prove useful to those similarly afflicted. About twelve years ago she complained of severe pains in her back and hip, which grew worse and worse until she was almost unable to move, or turn herself in bed. During this period her back and hip swelled very much, and the pain extended down the leg, which lost its natural power: a wasting of flesh - loss of appetite, and emaciation ensued, and her countenance depicted misery. She continued without much, if any alteration for the better, (keeping her strickly under the advice of an eminent medical gentleman) for a considerable time, when the swelling on the hip began to increase; her physician prescriptions became useless; they recommended the steel jacket - one was procured, tried, but in vain, and the disease seemed to bid defiance to all the well known remedies in that complaint, that were here employed. She was then considered as incurable. Her sister having died of the same complaint, after an illness of four years, we were of-opinion that Mary Ann must share the same fate. Having heard of the remarkable success of your Catholicon in scrofulous complaints, I was resolved to make a trial of it. She began its use, and in a few days the swelling on the hip broke, and discharged greatly; she could then use her crutches - in a few weeks longer her pains disappeared - the discharge ceased - the ulcer healed - her appetite returned - and her whole system resumed its wonted vigor. I believe, had your invaluable medicine been used when she first complained, it would have prevented her from being a cripple for the rest of her life. With many thanks for the benefits which my daughter has derived from the use of your Catholicon, I remain your respectable

The Maysville Eagle

Sir- I am now, thanks to your medicine, a hearty man. For nearly six years I have been a martyr to a disease whose ravages threatened, if not stopped, to put a period to my existence. Having had no regular medical advice from the commencement, my complaint at last got to such a height that I could not swallow without great pain and difficulty. Tumors formed in different parts of my body, and I began to think my situation almost desperate. The five bottles of Catholicon which I have taken completely cured me and I am now as well as I could wish to be. With my thanks, I am your obliged servant, & c. George Kane City of Philadelphia, ss. George Kane, of the district of Southward, personally appeared, and being duly sworn, doth declare and say, that the above statement is, in all respects, correct and true, and that the signature to it is in the hand writing of this deponent. . John Binns, Alderman. Philadelphia, May 28, 1824. Case. Samuel Rain, a stout, full grown lad of thirteen years of age, of healthy and robust habit of body, while swimming in the Delaware, some time in the month of June 1821, struck his shin bone a little below the knee against a boat - no pain nor unpleasant consequences resulted therefrom for the space of a week, when considerable inflammation and swelling ensued. Dr. S. a respectable physician of the neighborhood of Penn's neck, Salem county, New Jersey, where the boy resided, was called, and continued his attention for four years, during which time it grew worse and worse, until his uncle was seriously alarmed, being of opinion that the loss of his leg was the only means of saving his life. On the third day of August, 1824, he was put on a course of Potter's Vegetable Catholicon, and by its sole use is now completely restored. W.W. Potter. Attest - Samuel Rain. Certificate - Some time in August 1824, I was desired by W.W. Potter, to visit and examine the above lad, Samuel Rain - the disease he was afflicted with is termed Necosis, and a more severe case of it I never have seen - considerable portions of the whole diameter of the tibia, the main or shin bone of the leg had exfoliated and come out - the wound measuring at the time seven inches in length, extending from a little below the knee to near the ankle, two inches and a half in width, and two inches and a quarter in depth, the flesh being retroverted along the edges to the height of one inch and a half - he was much emaciated; had hectic fever; nightsweats; and was rapidly verging to the grave. In the state he was put on the Vegetable Catholicon, which in the course of three weeks, removed all the symptoms of hectic, and in the beginning of April, 1825, after using ten bottles of the medicine, he was discharged, cured. I have this day examined the limb - it is as sound as it was previous to the accident - a large quantity of healing boney matter filled up the vacuum by the exfoliated ... and the limb is as firm, and sound, and as useful as it could possibly be, had the accident never happened. Henry M'Murtrie, M. D. Philadelphia, May 16, 1816. I

The Maysville Eagle

do hereby certify, that twelve years ago, three days after being confined, both my legs began to swell, constituting the disease called Milk Leg About eight months after they commenced swelling they ulcerated; and in this deplorable state I continued till about one year since, when I began to use Potter's Vegetable Catholicon. By its sole use I am now perfectly well, the swelling is gone, the ulcers have healed and my limbs are as sound and healthy as ever. Margaret Hoffman. This is to certify, that my daughter, Elizabeth Binder, aged sixteen years, labored for twenty two months under a severe ulceration of the tongue and throat, which proceeded to such an extent as to eat away a third part of her tongue, and nearly to destroy her palate, and render her speech unintelligible. In this state, medical advice was resorted to, and every remedy that was suggested, tried, but in vain; when hearing of Mr. Potter's Vegetable Catholicon, was induced to try that: Two bottles have effectually cured her, and she is now perfectly well. Elizabeth Bender. Philadelphia, May 20, 1826. This is to certify, that my son, John Howorth, aged fourteen years, has been afflicted for eight years with the King's Evil; the best medical advice was had, and every remedy was tried, but without success, until Mr. Potter's Vegetable Catholicon was had recourse to, which has effectually cured him. The tumors are dispersed, and his general health is better than it has been for many years past. This I give unsolicited by Mr. Potter, and from a sincere desire of benefiting others who may be similarly situated. George Howorth. Justice of the peace Philadelphia County. Philadelphia, June 20, 1826. This is to certify, that I have been severely afflicted with the Rheumatism for the last fifteen years, and so bad that I was obliged to use crutches, or help, to enable me to move about. I tried every possible means of receiving relief from this deplorable situation, having used two bottles of Swaim's Genuine panacea without effect, when about a year since, I applied to Mr. W.W. Potter for a supply of his Vegetable Catholicon, and from the use of two bottles it has effected a cure and since I have stopped taking the medicine have, never enjoyed better health. Dorothy Bender. Philadelphia, June, 23, 1836 This is to certify, that I labored under a very severe Ulcerated sore throat and mouth, for upwards of a year and so desperate that it prevented my eating any thing of hard substance. I took three bottles of Swaim's Genuine Panacea without effect. In this state, hearing of Potter's Vegetable Catholicon, I had recourse to it, and by the use of three bottles have been effectually cured. It has been upwards of eighteen months since I ceased taking the medicine, and there is no appearance of return. Thomas Tomkins, Opposite Washington square. Philadelphia, April 1, 1826.

I saw the above case at the time he entered on the use of Mr. Potter's Catholicon, and can testify that it was a very severe and seemingly hopeless

The Maysville Eagle

one. I have seen the same person within a few days, and found him perfectly restored to health. H. M'Murtrie, M.D. April 9, 1826. I have labored under a very severe case of Tetter for the last five years, and in the course of that time was attended by two very respectable physicians of this city, who prescribed and recommended every popular remedy which they thought would prove of benefit, without success. I was blistered nine times on the face, and a course of mercury was proved ineffectually. At this time my situation became quite desperate, I was advised by my friends to try Potter's Vegetable Catholicon, in which they had great confidence, and finally consented to give it a trial. After using five bottles, the disease began to show itself more desperate than ever, which caused me to think I should never get freed from this desponding condition; but being urged by Mr. Potter to take more, (fully convincing me that his medicine would have the desired effect) I followed his advice, thank God, and from the use of nine bottles it effectually performed a cure. I am now perfectly well, my system having undergone a complete revolution. James Piper. This is to certify, that I have seen the above case and believe it to be true and correct. Wm. T. Carter. Philadelphia, Aug. 2, 1826. This is to certify, that I was afflicted with a disease in the liver for seven years, which produced a loss of appetite, and consequent emaciation. During this period I received the advice, and followed the prescriptions of Dr. H. and other physicians, without obtaining any relief. About twenty months past I applied to Mr. W. W. Potter, who advising a course of the Catholicon, I commenced taking it. Six bottles have effectually cured me, my appetite has returned, my pains are gone, and I now enjoy a state of the most perfect health. Martha M. M'Curdy.No. 76 Chesnut Street. Philadelphia, Aug. 3, 1826.

From the spring of 1822, until this summer, I was afflicted with Scrofula; every gland in my neck was affected by the rising of hard tumors, which broke and left deep ragged ulcers. I was under the care of three eminent practitioners at different times, who continued to prescribe for me about nine months, when my leg near the shin began to swell, which soon ulcerated - and a large ulcer also arose on my body; from the former proceeded a thick and offensive matter. I continued much in this state (my malady rather increasing,) for some months, and finding my physician's advice useless, I discharged them; and resorted to the use of Swaim's Genuine Panacea, which I persisted in to the extent of nine bottles, but without the slightest relief. Under these very unfavorable circumstances I commenced using Potter's Vegetable Catholicon, which soon manifested its influence over the disease; the tumor on my body now broke and began to discharge, and soon after all the ulcers began to heal very fast; in a few weeks more to my great astonishment the ulcers were entirely healed - the pains which I had been subject to, were removed - and my appetite restored

The Maysville Eagle

- and in fact my bodily health is very much improved from the exclusive use of Mr. Potter's Valuable Catholicon. Manual Morris. Philadelphia, September 26, 1826

Mr. W.W. Potter, Sir- I hereby give you a statement of my case, and you are at liberty to use it in any manner you may think proper. About four years ago I became afflicted with a complicated case of Scrofula and White Swelling, during this period I placed myself under the care of upwards of eighteen respectable physicians in Boston, Pittsburg, Albany and this place, but their prescriptions were in vain. My arm became useless, the elbow joint being very much enlarged, and so covered with ulcers, that my physician fearing a mortification would take place, advised me to submit to amputation, but this I rejected. On my back there was an ulcer as large as the palm of my hand, which became so painful that I despaired of ever being restored to health, or even getting relief. Having seen a similar case to my own which was cured by your valuable Catholicon, as the last resort I applied for it, and the happy result is, from its use for about three months - I am perfectly cured. John Healy. N.B. As I am about leaving this city, for information as to the accuracy of my case, several gentlemen of high respectability may be referred to. Philadelphia, May 28, 1824.

Sir- In consequence of imprudent exposure four years ago, I had the misfortune to become afflicted with a disease, the painful results of which induced me to apply in succession to several respectable physicians for this city, from whom, however, I received either no relief, or from whose remedies I received another complaint quite as distressing as the former. My whole system became affected. I could get no rest at night on account of the violent pain that I felt in every part of my body; the weakness and emaciation of which was such that I could scarcely walk. In this state I fortunately heard of your Vegetable Catholicon - four bottles of which completely restored me. I have now no pain, my appetite is good, and my strength restored. With many thanks for the relief your medicine has given me, I am, your obliged friend &c. William Wilson. Sworn and subscribed to before me. May 28, 1824. John Binns, Alderman.

(From the Darien (Geo.) Gazette, Nov.1) A most extraordinary cure effected by Potter's Cotholicon. Captain Donelly, keeper of the light on Sapelo and Master pilot for Doboy Bar, authorizes us to make known to the public the following fact of a recent date. "About a month ago, I bought three bottles of Potter's Catholicon, for the purpose of testing its virtues upon Mr. Peter M'Culloch, pilot of Doboy Bar, who had been for several years confined to his bed and crutches in consequence of diseased limbs, and ulcerated feet - the soles of his feet were in that shocking state, that the

The Maysville Eagle

bones were perceptible both to the sight and touch. Mr. M'Culloch after the use of three bottles of the Catholicon, laid aside his crutches and was this day in town attending to his business nearly perfect health." Darien, November 1, 1826.

Hartford Conn. Feb. 20 1827. Mr. Wm. W. Potter: Dear Sir - I have now but one bottle of Catholicon left. A person arrived this evening, who came sixty miles since morning, for 17 bottles of Catholicon, and would have taken 24, but I could let him have but nine. He came expressly for the article and says that the person who had used two bottles, has had a "liver affection or consumption" 20 years; and that three of the family are invalids, and have paid in ten years, for medical advice and medicine, $1,500. He says the person who used the two bottles, never found any medicine to compare with the Catholicon, and that the neighbors seeing the astonishing effects it produced a number of them sent the above person to procure the article, for various chronic diseases. The person told me he would wait two days, if he could procure the two dozen. Will you, without fail, send me, or if necessary, even come with a few boxes of the Catholicon to Hartford, as I fear delays will take place in New York and New

Bacon: Side pieces only wanted. Apply to Nat. Poyntz & Co. Maysville, July 4.

Cash or Salt. I will give forty cents per bushel for 10,000 bushels of Wheat, If delivered in my Steam Mill in all the months of July and August. Christian Shultz. Maysville, July 4.

Cash or Salt will be given for 30,000 bushels merchantable wheat, at forty cents per bushel, to be delivered in Christian Shultz's Steam Mill. Apply to Johnston Armstrong. Maysville, July 4.

Wheat. We will pay cash in hand, for 20,000 bushels of wheat. Delivered in our Steam Mill during the summer and fall. We will give forty cents per bushel from the shock, and we will receive it as soon as it becomes sufficiently dry to thresh. But as our market is fluctuating, our friends, our old customers, and the farmers generally, may do well to call on us before they sell, for though there may be many bidders in the market, we are determined to pay the highest cash price. We have a large supply of first rate salt on hand, which we will barter, as our custom is, at the lowest cash price, for wheat at the highest cash price. As usual, we will manufacture flour for our customers at the most reduced prices. N. & N. Hixon.

The Maysville Eagle

For sale, a likely Negro Woman, about 35 years of age, with her two children, one about seven, and the other three years old. Enquire of the printer.

August Election. Candidates for Congress. Gen. Thomas Metcalfe, Administr'n. Col. James Conn, for Jackson. State Senate. Robert Taylor, Esq. Adm's. Maj. Benjamin Bayles. State Legislature, for the administration: Adam Beatty, Esq. Capt. James Byers, Mr. David Morris. For Gen. Jackson: Mr. John Cowgill, William Worthington, Esq. Mr. James W. Bullock.

List of Letters, Remaining in the Post Office at Maysville, Ky. July 1st 1827. Mrs. A.M. Aston, Richard Applegate, Debora Armstrong, Edward Boone, Phineas S. Bryan, Ignatius Brawner, Wm. Byers (Ad.Co.), Mrs. Lydia Blair, Mrs. Eliz. J. Baldwin, Ste.T. Breckenridge, William Boyls, Joseph Budd, P.C. Brasher, Stephen Boyd (L.Co.), John Bland, James Berry, Garrison Baldwin(2) Edward Brewer, John G. Bacon, Wm Beatty or Saml. Wilson, William Brewer, John Bartley, George Brown (2), George W. Berry, Miss Alicia Cooke, James Chalfant, John Coe (Brown Co), John Chew, George W. Collins, Mrs. Agnes A. Collins, David Catlett, Abram Crookshanks, William Carpenter, Miss Elizabeth Catlett, Oliver Cahil, Hugh Copper, Mrs. Mary Clark, George Corwine, Evin Campbell or Jeremiah Martin, Nicholas Dennis, John N. Davis, John Duzan, Richard Dye, Benjamin Davis, Wm.B. Derrett, Joseph Davis (2) Charles Dougherty, Isaac Dollis, Miss Elizabeth Duell, Abraham Duzan, James Easton, Mrs. Min. Etherington, Gillespie Jos. (Le. Co.) Thomas Grover, William Gilbert, Nathan Gilbert, jr. Capt. John Hall, Mrs. Nancy Housley, Mrs. Nancy Holley, Stephen Holley, Nathan Hukill, Mrs. Sarah Ham, Alexander Harrover, Law. Van Hollinback, Dennis B. Hoblitzell, Gilbert Hall, William Hayden, John Nancy, Miss Isabella Hiett (Brown Co.O.), Miss Mary Ann Isrel, P.B. Jones, Moses Justice, Peter January, Mrs. Maria Johns, Thomas Kerr(2), Mrs. Rebecca Kendal, William Kerlin, James Litefoot, Mr. Langley, Mrs. Lucinda Lamb, Isaac Lewis, John Mortimore, Nathl. Medaugh (2), Maj. Thos. Marshall, Hugh M'Connell, George Maple, Jeremiah Martin, Jacob Mower (2), Mrs. S. M'Clung, John A. M'Clung, John M'Cauley, Jesse Middleswarth, Edwin Mathews, William Mason, James Meenach, John M'Knon, Thomas McKinsey, Reuben Marshall, David Maple (Le.Co), Patrick May, Benjamin More, Achesheth Miller, William Newsum, Jesse Nash, Henry Ortkeiss, Joseph Orsler, Dr. Geo. M. Payne, Benjamin Pollard, Robert Payne, Samuel Pilkington, Caleb Peddleord, James Pemberton, Danl.

The Maysville Eagle

Parker (Br.Co), Elias Pointer (Ad. Co.), Eli Plummer, Henry Rains, Elizabeth Rumford, John M. Raulston, S. Reeves, Richard K. Rushton, Geo H. Sinclair, (3), Capt. Chaun. Shepard, Ezra Spencer, Daniel Swearingen, John Sullivan, Edward Shaddows, Samuel Stillwell, Rev. J. Stamper, James Scott, Presley Stephenson, Moses Thomas, Cornelius Threikeld, Josith Tomson, Miss Sarah Tiffee, Eli Vaughn or Mrs. Mary Nash, James R. Wilson, jr. James Willett, Charles A. Wood, Jesse Wood, Miss Sarah Wright, Daniel Wood or John Lambs, Handable Willett. William Murphy, P.M.

Stone Cutting. The undersigned respectfully informs the citizens of Maysville and the surrounding country, that he has commenced stone cutting, in the small brick row on Third Street near Messers. Hixson's Steam Mill. He has a large assortment of the best free stone on hand and will shortly be supplied with marble. Tombstones and head and foot stones will be handsomely cut and lettered to order - and the business in all its various branches shall be industriously attended to and all orders for work received a speedily and faithful attention. John Nash. Maysville, July 4.

Wanted. A manager to take charge of a Rope Walk. Liberal wages will be given to one properly qualified and of sober, industrious habits. Apply to the subscriber in Washington, Mason County, Ky. Milton Taylor. June 13, 1827

Gabriel's Lick Springs, Lewis County, Ky. The undersigned respectfully informs the public, that he is now prepared at the White Sulphur Spring, on his farm, six miles east of Williamsburg, in Mason County, to accommodate a few families with private rooms- and pledges himself to spare no pains to promote the comfort and convenience of those who may favor him with a call. This spring is considered by those who have tested its qualities, to possess very nearly the same medicinal virtues of Drennon's Lick Spring, in Henry County, which contains, principally sulphurated hydrogen and carbonic acid gasses, sulphur, sulphate and muriate of soda, and sulphate of magnesia, besides a small quantity of some other qualities. The water is believed to be highly beneficial in dispeptic complaints, hypochrondrack gout, chronic rheumatism, eruptions of the skin in general, old ulcers and the diseases peculiar to females of delicate constitutions. Asahel Brewer. Lewis Co. Ky., June 20, 1827.

Hord & Browning's Patent Flour. Obtained patent on 12th March, 1825.

The Maysville Eagle
White Sulphur and Chalybeate Springs. Lewis County, Kentucky. The subscriber takes this method of informing his friends and the public in general, that he is prepared for the reception of visitors, and pledges himself that no exertion shall be wanting on his part, to render to his visitors and guest every accommodation in his power. His charges will be $3 per week for board. Peter T. January.

Washington Hall, Washington, Ky. John Rankins, has taken the large and very commodious brick building in Washington, Mason County, Ky. Lately known as the banking house of the Washington Branch Bank, and most recently occupied as a Tavern by Mr. Hord, where he has opened a House of Entertainment and solicits the patronage of his friends and the public - assuring them that no... shall be spared to render complete satisfaction to all who may give him a call. June 13, 1827.

Wednesday July 18, 1827

Oration by Benjamin F. Reeve, at the celebration of the 4^{m} of July at Mr. Gates, in Mason County. A lengthy speech with political views.

From the Lexington Reporter. Extract of text. The dinner to Mr. Clay. On Thursday last, the proposed Dinner was given to Mr. Clay at Noble's, by the citizens of Lexington and Fayette county. At 11 o'clock , Capt. Bledsoe's troop of Calvary from Athens, and a number of citizens on horseback, waited upon Mr. Clay at his lodgings in town, and escorted him to the place of dining. The escort was conducted by Maj. Robb who acted as Marshall of the day, at the request of the committee of arrangements. On arriving at Noble's tho' at an early hour an immense number of Mr. C's old friends, many of them the first acquaintances formed by him in the state, were found already assembled and eagerly pressed around their old and faithful public servant, to welcome him, and to renew their pledges of undiminished confidence and esteem. The number present was computed by the committee at 1500; other think the number greater, we are satisfied it could not have been much less. The Hon. W. R. Rochester, and several strangers from a distance were invited guest. .... A very handsome address was delivered after dinner, by Mr. William Bullock..... The Rev. C.W. Cloud asked a blessing at the table. ....Col. AB Bowman acted as President. Capt. John Fowler, Capt. John Postlethwait, Dr. Pindell, A.E. Price and Richard Higgins, Esquires as Vice Presidents. Volunteer toast. By Judge Hickey. Kentucky - distinguished by the valor, the patriotism and the eloquence of her sons - May she never lack either of those high qualities to maintain her rights and animate her efforts and vindicate her

The Maysville Eagle

honor. By Charles H. Wickliffe. Henry Clay - The statesman and Orator, may his commanding talents and great exertions in the cause of Internal Improvements and domestic manufactures, elevate him to the highest office in the gift of a free people. By W.B. Rochester. Kentucky - Conspicuous in devotion to the American System, in sustaining her distinguished Statesman who has so triumphantly vindicated its policy, she not only is true to herself, but advances the best interest of the nation. By Moses L. Miller of Georgetown. My little factory I have stopped this day; That I might come and honor Henry Clay. By Mr. A.F. Hawkins. Henry Clay it is not the ravings of his personal enemies nor the writings of disappointed political aspirants that can destroy our confidence in the integrity of our faithful public servant. By John B. Coreman, The roads and those who travel them - May the first be Mac-Adamised, and the last Adamised on a good Clay foundation. By Maj. G.C. Thompson of Mercer. The "still small voice" from Monticello - May our happy Republic never, no never, "follow the fate of all others, and fall under Military Rule." By G.W. Anderson. The sun of Jack is rising, but Jackson is setting. By Capt. M'Kinney. Unanimity and prosperity at home - friendship and peace abroad. By Wm. Easthem. Domestic Manufactures and internal improvements - The only course to national wealth and honor.

Virginia State Navigation Lottery. Highest Prize 5,000 dollars...Aug. Leftwich, Manager

Long letter to the paper about the Wool and Woolens Bill by A. Beatty.

The Hon. J. S. Johnston, senator in Congress from the State of Louisiana, arrived in Maysville on Monday last, and is now at the residence of his father, Dr. John Johnston, of Washington.

Judge Johnston and Judge Rochester, (the former a native and the latter for several years a resident of this county,) have been invited and will attend the dinner to be given to Mr. Clay, in Maysville on this day.

We are authorized to announce Mr. Thomas Robinson as a candidate for the Senate of Kentucky from Mason County.

Baltimore, June 29. It gives us pleasure to be enabled to state, that Col. Long, Capt. McNeil and Dr. Howard, of the corps of Topographical Engineers have arrived in Baltimore prepared to enter upon the examination of the country between this city and the Ohio, preparatory to commencing the necessary surveys, in order to enable the board of

The Maysville Eagle

directors to determine upon the final location of the Baltimore and Ohio Road.....

Early Marriage. Married in Montgomery county Illinois, 10^{m} June, Master John Parish, aged fifteen to Miss Libins Goodwin, aged sixteen. This is carrying the advice of Dr. Franklin to marry in the morning of life, to its ultimatum. We do not know which here to admire most, the discretion of the friends, or the tender and steadfast love of the parties themselves. They seem to have been seized with a laudable desire to people the wild prairies of Illinois.

Insurrection of slaves in Georgia. A letter from Georgia to a gentleman in this city, dated June 6, 1827, says "A most dangerous and extensive insurrection of the blacks was detected at Macon a few days since. They banded together to the number of 300, and supposed to be instigated and headed by a French emigrant from the Mississippi. His slaves were in the plot. They had only arrested one of the rebels. The whole of the others with the Frenchman have made their escape."

Marriage. On Thursday evening last, by the Rev. Walter Warder, Col Stark Fielder, of Louisville to Miss Mary Dye, daughter of Mr. John Dye Sen. Of Mason County.

Boot & Shoe Making. James Saffern, Begs leave to inform the citizens of Washington and of Mason County generally, that he has commenced the above business in the white frame building one door north of Benjamin Bayles' Hatter Shop, in Washington where all orders for work shall be promptly and faithfully attended to and where he solicits the custom of the public. Three or four journeymen are wanted at his manufactory. To good workmen, and moral men, constant employment and liberal wages will be given. Washington, July 18.

Thomas Tebbs, Foushee Tebbs, Willoughby Tebbs, Samuel Tebbs, John Spencer and Mary his wife, late Mary Tebbs, and the heirs of Margaret Triplett, whose maiden name was Tebbs, and who are heirs of Willoughby Tebbs, deceased; and William L. Thompson and Eliza his wife, late Massie, Nathaniel Massie, Richard Massie, Ann Massie and Henry Massie, who are heirs of Henry Massie, deceased and Walter Dunn: Take Notice. That on the second Monday in August next, at the office of Walker Reid, attorney at law, in Washington, Mason County, Ky. We shall take the depositions of Col. Alexander D. Orr, Col. Marshall Key, Capt. Thomas Young, and Walker Reid, Esq. As evidence in the suit in chancery, depending in the

The Maysville Eagle

Mason circuit court, in which we are complainants, and you and others are defendants; and if we shall not be able to finish on that date we shall continue over until the next day and complete the taking. Septimus D. Clarke, John Shackleford, for himself and his co. heirs. July 18, 1827

List of Letters remaining in the post office in Washington on the 20th June 1827. If not taken out in three months from this date They will be sent to the General Post office as dead letters. William Bogle, B. Bayless, James M. Bush, Robert C. Burroughs, Capt. Phil'n Burgess, Wilis Ballenger, Gen. David Chiles, Hannah Chambers, Geo. Chinn, Sally Crittenden, Jacob Cockenhover, Paul Durrett,2, Jacob Davis, Walter Duncan, Joseph Duncan, J.C.Dewees, Gov. Joseph Desha, Jacob W.H. Ely, John Edwards, Perry Fiffe, Arthur Fox, Samuel Gifford, Edward Groves, Erasmus Gill, Wm. Henry, E.B. Hanigan, Thomas Hale, Elizabeth Houghton, Francis T. Hord, Benj. Johnson or Francis T. Hord, Nelson Knight, Harriet Key, Isham Key, Walter Lacy, Rev. Fran. Landrum, Mrs. Lamby, Charles Lee, Rebecca Moody, Thomas Marshall, John Marshall, Arthur G. M'Cann, Richard Mitchell or Col. John Pickett, David Morrison, Richard Mattony, Alexander D. Orr, James O'Cull, Elizabeth Oneil. Phillip Palmer, Thomas Payne, John N. Payne, John Rankins, Deborah Ramy, E. Roper, Elizabeth D. Rist, R. Smather, Margaret Smith, Sherrif Mason County, Francis Shinn, J.D. Taylor, Jacob Thomas, John Tabb, Enos Woodward, Daniel Wood, David Wood, Robert Walton or Edward Robertson, Josiah Wilson, John Weiden or Mrs. Mary Franklin, Elizabeth T. Wilson, Wm. H. Wilson, John Wallingsford, Richard Wood. John Green, P.M.

For Sale, A likely Negro Woman, about 35 years of age, with her two children, one about seven, and the other three years old. Inquire of the Printer.

Maysville, Ky. Wednesday Nov. 29, 1837

A Scene in a Private Mad-House. Poem by M. G. Lewis, Esq.

From Washington Irving's Adventures in the Rocky Mountains. On the 17th of July, a small brigade of fourteen trappers, led by Milton Sublette, brother of the captain, set out with the intention of proceeding to the south-west. They were accompanied by Sinclair and his fifteen free trappers; Captain Wythe, also and his New England band of beaver hunters and salmon fishers, now dwindled down to eleven, took this opportunity. Long extract. Names mentioned Antoine Goin, a half breed son of an Iroquois hunter

The Maysville Eagle

who had been cruelly murdered by the Black Feet. A friend named Campbell.

Horse Shoe Iron. Warranted to be of a superior quality, just received and for sale by Gaylord & Co.

H. Taylor, Attorney at Law. Will attend to any professional business in the Mason, Fleming, Bracken, Lewis & Greenup Circuit Courts. His office is in the one formerly occupied by M'Clung in Washington, Ky. Oct. 4, 1837

Virginia Tobacco A few boxes on hand and for sale by Clarke & Ryan. April 5, 1837

Removal. Doctor G. Dunhar. Has removed his office to Third Street, and established himself in the small frame building formerly occupied by and generally known as Dr. Coburn's office; where he will be gratified to receive the continued patronage of his friends and the public. Maysville, Nov. 1, 1837.

Lost on Second Street, between Ash and Short streets, on Thursday evening A Bead Purse, containing a three dollar note, a 25 cent silver piece, a gold breast pin, and an account on Robert Payne, Esq. For the sum of eight dollars. On one side of the purse is the representation of a dog, and on the other several Greek letters. The finder will be suitably rewarded by leaving the purse and contents at the Eagle Book Store. Maysville, Oct. 21, 1837.

Glass-ware just received. J. W. Johnston & Co. Druggist.

Cordage. Grass rope, bed, cords, plough lines & c. on hand and for sale by Clarke & Ryan. Maysville, Feb. 8, 1837

G. W. Evens, Surgeon Dentist, next door to Mrs. Goddards Hotel, where he will perform all operations of his profession in the neatest manner. Teeth inserted, separated, plugged, cleansed, or extracted in the neatest manner. Ladies can be waited upon at their residences.

Hollow Glassware. January & Huston

Dr. J. W. Henry, Having permanently located himself in Washington, respectfully tenders his professional service to the citizens of that place and its vicinity. His is one door above the one recently occupied by Dr. Owens.

The Maysville Eagle

Administrator's Notice. The sale bonds of the estate of Ezekial Forman, will be due the 10th of November. Of all those who pay punctually, ... bank paper will be received. . of those .. not specie will be demanded. We must .. close, as the estate owes some debts which must me paid. The notes will be at the store ... Thos. S. Forman and others Administrators. Oct 11, 1837

One Cent Reward. Ranaway from the subscriber living in Nicholas County, Ky. An indented apprentice to the Wagon Making Business, by the name of David A. Weever, about 20 years of age, 5 feet 6 or 7 inches high, light hair and tolerably fair skin. At some times he has a stammering in his speech, will weight about 100 and 25 or 30 pounds. I do hereby forewarn any person or persons from harboring or employing said boy, as I am fully determined to put the law in force against any person or persons for the said offense. I will give the above reward for said boy if taken either in the state or out of it. John Matchet.

Bourbon Whisky. 200 bbls. Whiskey now receiving for sale by J.. B. M'Ilvain.

Cross Cut and Mill Saws. For sale a lot first rate crosses cut and mill saws. January & Huston. Maysville

Pearl Ash. 1000 lbs. Just received per steamer. Huntress for sale low by J. W. Johnston & Co.

Dye Stuffs. Just received from New Orleans. W. R. Wood

Almanacs for the 1838. Loomis Pittsburgh Almanacs, Magazines and single for 1838, by the gross dozen or single; for sale by Edward Cox. .

$500 Reward. I will give the above reward for the apprehension & delivery of a murderer by the name of Tolbert Ernest in the Bowling Green Jail, Warren County, Ky. Said Ernest is about 22 years of age, 5 feet 8 or 10 inches high, with fair skin, blue eyes and a very bad countenance; is fond of gambling at cards and dice, and is very profane in conversation. He was brought up in Simpson County, Ky. where he committed the murder. He has been in the habit of attending the races in all the adjoining counties and at Nashville Ten, and has been at New Orleans two or three times. George H. Holland. Nov. 10, 1837

The Maysville Eagle

Tho's Y. Payne, Attorney at Law, Maysville Kentucky, Will hereafter regularly attend the Circuit Courts throughout the entire 1st Judicial District, and solicits business in the counties of Greenup, Fleming, Bracken, Lewis and Mason. His office is in Maysville, next door to his residence, on Main Cross Street, between Front, and Second Streets. February 2, 1836

Dr. Duke, Will continue to devote his entire attention to the several branches of his profession. His office is the one he has heretofore occupied opposite the Insurance Office. Night calls will be made at Mr. Morton's residence. March 1, 1838.

The boot makers. The subscriber having been appointed agent for the sale of E.G. Pomerroy's patent horizontal boot clamps, or crimping boots, begs leave to offer an article for the use of the craft; that will produce the most perfect elastic front, with a great saving of stock and labor. They will be exhibited at my shop in Maysville, and sold on the most reasonable terms. The craft are particularly invited to examine for themselves. P. Carpenter. Maysville, March 13, 1837.

Doctors Taliaferro & Pickett, have associated themselves in the practice of Physic, Surgery & c. and offer their united attention to all cases in which they may be consulted, either in the town or vicinity. Office on Front Street, a few doors above Dudley's Hotel. Maysville, June 10, 1837.

Dissolution of Partnership. The partnership heretofore existing under the firm of Nathan Davis & Co. is this day dissolved by mutual consent. All debts due the firm will be paid to Nathan Davis, and all debts due by the firm will be also paid by Nathan Davis. Sept 30, 1837. Nathan Davis, James C. Davis. Maysville, Oct. 11, 1837

Valuable Property for sale. The subscriber proposes to sell his valuable steam saw mill, to which is annexed one run of stone, together with a tract of land, containing 256 acres, situated on the waters of Buchanan in the county of Fleming, 4 miles S. West of Elizaville, between the road leading to the Lower Blue Lick and the state road; one mile and a quarter from the former and three quarters from the latter. Said tract and the circumlacent county teem with good timber admirably adapted to the manufacture of plank. The Engine and Mill are new, having been in operation but one year, and the situation is a most excellent one for the location of an extensive distillery there being sufficiency of water for the operation during the entire year. The subscriber also wishes to sell a wagon and team of two

The Maysville Eagle

yoke oxen, timber wheels and other necessary appendages. Any person wishing to purchase will please call and examine for themselves. Hiram Metcalfe. April 19, 1837

Valuable real estate for sale. Wishing to leave the city.... One home and lot running from Second to Third Streets, on which is also a Blacksmith Shot and Plough Shop. One unimproved lot, fronting Second Street 41 feet and running back 133 feet. One Farm, one mile from the city, fronting Limestone creek, containing one hundred three and a half acres, under cultivation, well cultivated and is well calculated for raising stock, as it has 12 good springs on it. Also, one other farm, in Fleming County, adjoining Fielder's mill on Johnson's Fork, containing one hundred thirty-one and a half acres - sixty of which is cleared, the balance well timbered and situated immediately on the Maysville and Lexington Turnpike Road. Apply to Wm. C. Newdigate June 1, 1836

Superior Cotton Yarns, R. H. Lee, having very much enlarged his Cotton Mill, by new and improved machinery, from Paterson, New Jersey, and placed it under the management of experienced superintendent - the undersigned will be pleased to supply the orders of city dealers and country merchants with warranted years, at the Pittsburgh prices. R. H. Lee & W. Rees. Maysville, Feb 16, 183?

Valuable Farm for sale. The undersigned offer for sale the farm belonging to the estate of E. Forman, dec'd lying two miles East of Mayslick, on the Upper Blue Lick Road, containing 370 acres. The land is equal to any in the county in fertility - and is new in a state of high cultivation. If sold before the middle of March, immediate possession will be given. Purchasers are requested to examine the land. J. S. Forman & others, Adm'rs. February 15, 1837.

Fulling Notice. The undersigned hereby informs the public that he has made arrangements for the receiving and delivering of cloths, with the following gentlemen as his agents viz:: Conquest Owens of Washington, Mr. George L. Forman of Lewisburg and Mr. James Alexander of the House of H. Durret & Co. Flemingsburg, Ky. Cloths with directions as to the particular manner of finishing, left at either of the above places will be promptly attended to. Dressed and returned with dispatch. Henry Green. Brodrick's Mill, Mason Count Kentucky. October 18, 1837

Bracken Sct. Taken up by James Nicholas, living on the river bottom, about one mile above Augusta. One Bay Mare, with a star and snip in her

The Maysville Eagle

forehead, both hind feet white, her fore feet indicate that she has been badly foundered, a little crease fallen on the weathers, fourteen hands three inches high, supposed to be six years old last spring. No other marks or brands perceivable; appraised to forty five dollars before me, a Justice of the Peace for said county, on the 26th day of August 1837. J. T. M'Kibben, J.P.B.C.

F.T. Hord, attorney at Law, Maysville, Ky. Will regularly attend the courts of this circuit and the Court of Appeals. Maysville, Sept. 7, 1837

Pocket Book Lost. Lost, on Limestone Creek, between Henry Bolinger's and Robert Wilson's on Thursday night the 2nd instant, a small red Morocco Pocket Book. With a steel clasp containing $78 in bank notes - all on the Maysville Branch Bank of Kentucky, except one three dollar note, a five dollar gold piece, one note of hand for $40 on Thos. Williams, executed the 1st of September, on note, just paid off, given by me with my father as surety, to Joseph Rumford for $370 12 ½ - together with a gold ring. The finder shall be liberally rewarded by leaving the pocket book and its contents at the Eagle Book Store, or handing it to the subscriber at his father's residence on Limestone Creek. William Wilson, Nov 8, 1837.

Doctor John Shackleford, Will continue to practice Medicine, surgery and obstetrics. He pledges his expertise to give satisfaction to those who may require his professional services. Office 2nd Street, two doors below the corner of 2nd and Marke (sic) Streets. Maysville, Sept. 14, 1836

Medical Notice. S. Avard, Botanic Physician, offers his professional services to the citizens of Maysville, and its vicinity. Having had great success in his former practice, Dr. Avard feels a confidence in soliciting a share of the patronage of the citizens of Mason County. His medicines are prepared entirely of vegetable substances in a highly concentrated state, and thus adapted to any forms of disease incident to the human frame. N.B. Office in 2nd street, in the house recently occupied by Mrs. Green. Nov. 8, 1837.

A call. We respectfully request those who are indebted to us, to call and make payment of their accounts by the 20th of this month, as we are desirous of starting east for a supply of goods. We avail ourselves of this opportunity to say to our friends and the public, that we have on hand, a cheap and well assorted stock of merchandise, and can sell upon as reasonable terms as any house in the west. Taylor & Green. Washington Aug. 2, 1837

The Maysville Eagle

Notice to Contractors, Sealed proposals will be received until Saturday, the 11th inst. For the construction of one half mile of the Maysville and Bracken Turnpike Road, beginning at the west end of Second Street of Maysville. Proposals to be deposited with the Trustees, at the store room of J. S. & W. Chambers. C. Shultz, Pres. M & B.T.P.R. Co. Maysville, Nov 8, 1837

Ranaway from the subscribers, on Saturday night last, the 14th instant, a Negro Man, named Lewis, aged about 28 or 30 years, about 5 feet 4 or 5 inches high, thick upper lip and turns up the corner of it when speaking, does not speak very distinctly, has a humble manner when spoken to. He has on, we believe, a frock cloth coat and fur cap, no other clothing known. He is a hempspinner and has waited in the house, and he may make application for employment in one of the pursuits. We will give one half of the amount for which he will sell, for his apprehension and delivery to us. Thos. & Geo. Forman. Mason Co. Oct. 19, 1837.

A long torn article mentioning "My old Friend Zeikel Bigelow" by J. Downing, Major, Downingville Militia, 2nd Brigade.

For New Orleans. Steam Boat Conqueror, Capt. J. Moore, Will be at Maysville about the first of December, preparatory for a trip to New Orleans. The Conqueror is a new a splendid boat, of 500 tons, and can accommodate, in superior style, a large number of passengers, for freight or passage, apply to January & Huston. Maysville, Nov. 17, 1837

Tallow Wanted. 10 cts. A pound given for Tallow, in groceries, and $2.50 a bushel for mustard seed. Eggs, butter & lard purchased at the market price, at Stickney & Co's wholesale and retail grocery, Sutton Street, (lately occupied by P. Throop & Son.)Nov. 8, 1837

For Sale. In the town of Murphysville, A House and Lot, a small well finished farm house, a good situation for a mechanic. Terms very reasonable. For further information call and see the subscriber. George Miley. Murphysville, Nov. 25, 1837

Johnston's Vermafuge. For expelling worms, a valuable article - For sale by J. W. Johnston & Co

Liquors for sale. W & N. Poyntz. .

The Maysville Eagle

Cranberries. 11 bbls. Fresh cranberries, just received and for sale by Wm. Parker. Maysville, Nov. 1, 1837

Notice. All those indebted to the undersigned, either by note or book account, are requested to make payment immediately, as longer indulgence cannot be given. Thomas Steers. Mason Co. Sept. 20, 1837

Notice. I have on hand, two thousand yards janes, at different qualities, manufactured on hand looms, much of it very heavy, suitable for Negro clothes. I will barter for clean wool or sell very low for cash. A supply will be kept always on hand. Isaac Lewis. Lewisburg, Sept. 23, 1837

Fulling and cloth dressing. The undersigned respectfully informs the public, that he has taken the well known establishment of Mr. James Brodrick, 2 ½ miles north of Washington, and 2 south west of Maysville, on Lawrence's Run, where he will be prepared to do all kinds of coloring, fulling & cloth dressing, with neatness and dispatch. The establishment is now fitted up and will be ready for the fall rains. From his experience in, and his attention to business, he hopes to merit and receive a liberal share of public patronage. Henry Green. Oct. 4, 1837

Jeans & Sattinetts. A large supply of jeans and sattinetts, ofrious (sic) qualities, for sale low, on liberal credits by R. Buchanan. Cincinnati, Sept. 9, 1837

For sale A Negro Woman, who is a good cook and washer - inquire at the Eagle Book Store. Maysville, Sept. 27, 1837

New Candle and Soap factory. The undersigned informs the citizens of Maysville and the contiguous counties that he has just established at the new bridge on Limestone Creek, A soap & candle factory, where he will manufacture and keep constantly on hand, every variety of soap, of a superior quality, and candles, which he will warrant equal to any sold in the market. Locating himself here as an entire stranger, he is aware that the quality of his articles, must recommend him - and determined to spare no pains or expense to make them of a very superior quality, he respectfully solicits public patronage. Tallow, soap, grease, and ashes purchased at the market price, for cash, or soap and candles. Jacob Bacon. Maysville, Sept 27, 1837

Notice. The undersigned having associated with him, Thomas Porter and William Hodge in the business of manufacturing bagging and bale rope, the

The Maysville Eagle

business will be conducted in future under the name and firm of Shultz, Porter & Hodge. Christian Shultz. Cash will be given for a few crops of good hemp. Maysville, Oct. 4, 1837

Copartnership, the undersigned have formed a co-partner ship, under the name and firm of Artus & Metcalfe, and opened (in the house lately occupied by E.F. Metcalfe) a house for the acting a General Agency & Commission Business. Where they are prepared to receive store, forward and sell merchandise of every description. Their Warehouse is secure and convenient, and they pledge themselves to transact any business entrusted to their care, with promptitude and fidelity. They will keep an assortment of groceries constantly on hand, and will sell at the lowest markets prices. James Artus, E.F. Metcalfe.

To the public, E. F. Metcalfe returns his grateful acknowledgments to those who have so kindly supported him, for the last two years, and respectfully invites a continuance with the firm of Artus & Metcalfe. He avails himself of this opportunity to say all those having unsettled accounts are requested to call and adjust the same. E. F. Metcalfe. Oct. 25, 1837

Anvils. Just received and for sale by Gaylord & Co. February 18, 1837

Maysville, Wednesday, November 29, 1837

To Col. Stephen Lee. For years you have served us in various subordinate stations with unquestioned zeal and Fidelity. We all know you - all acknowledge your firmness and integrity- and as a testimonial of our regard for you as a man, and approbation of your conduct as an officer, we are anxious to bestow upon you our suffrages for the office of Mayor at the next election. Should it be consistent with your feelings to suffer your name to be used as a candidate for that of ?, you will find rally to your support. Many old friends.

Temperance convention. A convention of the Temperance Societies of Northern Kentucky, met in the Methodist Episcopal Church of this city on yesterday at 11 O'clock. The convention was organized by the election of Captain Charles Ward of Mason County, President. The other officers, with the proceedings will be given hereafter. About forty delegates are in attendance.

Democracy A barely readable letter which ends with I called at the Post office in Maysville, this day the 25th Nov. for a letter, the price was 18 ½

The Maysville Eagle

cents, for which I offered 12 ½ in specie and 6 ½ in a Shin Plaster, but was refused, and had to go home to get the silver to buy my letter. This makes me think all is not right and that there is something rotten in Denmark and that I must be disappointed in the name, and do now renounce it. Yours with respect. James Phillips, a known democrat.

Honorable Distinction The Philadelphia Herald states that Peter S. Duponceau, Job R. Tyson and Daniel M. Keim (late of Reading) have been elected honorary members of Roy's Society of Northern Antiquities at Copenhagen: They have each published to the society giving an account of the discovery of this continent by some Norwegian navigators, as early as the 12th century.

Mr. Calhoun said last winter, that the administration party was "united only by the centripetal power of plunder" We wonder if Mr. C. had then a suspicion, that this "centripetal power of plunder" would in less then twelve months draw him into the party! Louisville. Journ.

Gen. Robert Y. Hayne, the distinguished resident of the Cincinnati & Charleston Rail Road Co. addressed the two houses in convention, last evening, on the character and claims of the great work in which he is deeply engaged. At five o'clock he gave way for a motion to adjourn, and will resume his remarks at 10 o'clock this morning. The spacious hall of the House of Representatives was crowded to excess, and the concourse of spectators included a large number of ladies - Nashville Banner, Nov. 20

In Washington City, on the morning of the 17th instant, Mrs. Ellen Pickett, consort of Col. James C. Pickett, Fourth Auditor of the Treasury, and second daughter of the Ex-Governor Desha, of Kentucky, in the 37th year of her age. Mrs. P. was a native of Mason county, in which she spent the greater part of her life, and her numerous friends in the region will hear of her death with unfeigned regret. Possessing a strong and highly cultivated mind - amiable courteous and kind - her house was the home of refined social enjoyment and true Kentucky hospitality. She sedulously cultivated the domestic virtues and found the society of her husband, and in the instruction of her children, her highest sources of enjoyment. On them, the affective dispensation falls most heavily, for although time may mitigate the intensity of their grief, it can never repair their loss. But few persons have descended to the grave more generally and sincerely beloved, or whose memory will be more fondly cherished.

The Maysville Eagle

Lottery Intelligence. Lottery tickets for sale by J. G. Kendrick. Maysville Corner of Front and Sutton Streets. Maysville, Nov 29, 1837.

Dissolution. The partnership of McCardle and Ryan is this day dissolved by mutual consent. Persons indebted to the firm can make payment to Messrs. Clarke & Ryan, who are authorized to receive all money due, receipt for the same and .. any unsettled business of said firm. W. H. McCardle, H. M. Ryan. Maysville, Nov. 28th, 1837

Public Notice. Our co-partnership expires by limitation on the 1st of January, 1838. It will be continued as heretofore; but it is absolutely necessary that our accounts should be closed up to that period. The indulgence we have extended to many of our customers, justifies the belief, that our friends will meet with promptitude this request. R. H. Lee & W. Rees. Maysville, 28, 1837

Dissolution. The firm of L. Perry & Co. was this day dissolved by mutual consent. The business will hereafter be conducted by Lewis Perry, who is authorized to settle the business. Sarah Richardson, Lewis Perry, Nov. 29, 1837

Commission House, New Orleans, the subscribers have associated themselves under the firm of Ogden & Southgate, for the purpose of transacting a general Commission and Forwarding Business in the city of New Orleans and are now prepared to receive consignments Samuel C. Ogden, Richard H. Southgate,

Sale of Real Estate in Mayslick KY. By virtue of a decree of the Mason Circuit Court, lately rendered upon a petition filed by myself, as guardian for the infant heirs of Charles Linthicum deceased. I will, upon the 1st day of January 1839, offer for sale at public auction, two lots, situated in that village, which descended from Charles Linthicum to his heirs. One of the lots that upon which the Tavern House, now occupied by David Bassett is situated, (being the best tavern stand in the place, with a very superior stable,) the other an unimproved back lot. The lots will be shown to the bidders on the day of the sale. The sale will be on a credit of one and two years, the purchaser giving bond with approved security for the purchase money, bearing interest from the date. A deed in pursuance of the decree under which I am acting will be made to the purchaser, conveying all the interest of the heirs of Charles Linthicum deceased. Hiram Baker, Com'r. Nov 29, 1837.

The Maysville Eagle

Administrator's Notice. Notes given at the sale of the estate of E. Forman, deceased, were due the 10th Nov. We will expect them all settled before the 10th December next; all unsettled thereafter will be at once sued upon. J. S. Forman & others, Adm's Washington Nov 29, 1837

Watches and Jewelry. The subscriber announces to his friends and the public generally, that he has removed his establishment one door above Mortan & Proctor's store, where he has just received and opening a handsome assortment of Watches and Jewelry. He invites the ladies and gentlemen to call and examine his stock, as he feels assured they will find the variety as great as is usually kept in such establishments. He is also prepared to repair watches of every description in the best manner, and warrant them to perform. J.S. Gilpin. Maysville, Nov. 25, 1837

A bargain. A bargain. J.S. & W. Chambers, being desirous of closing their business offer their entire stock of goods for sale, on terms highly profitable. The stock consists of about $12,000 worth of dry goods well assorted, which have been selected with care for the retail business. Those wishing to purchase will do well to apply speedily as we are disposed to make the terms advantageous, both as to price and time. Application can be made to us at Maysville or to W. B. Phillips at Louisville. If not sold by the 5th of December we will proceed to sell at cost for cash. N. B. all those indebted to J. S. & W. C. are requested to call and close their accounts as soon as practicable. Maysville, Nov. 25, 1837.

Notice. The books for subscriptions of stock in the Eutaw House company, will be opened on Monday, the 4th day of December next, at the office of the Maysville Insurance company, and will be kept open until there shall be sufficient stock taken to enable the company to organize and make preparations for the improvements contemplated in the charter of said company. W.M. Mackey, R.H. Lee, Wm. M. Poyntz, Thos. Y. Payne, James N. Morrison, Francis T. Hord, John M. Morton, Com'rs. Nov. 25, 1837

Dissolution. The firm of Calvert, Wallingford & Co. has been dissolved by mutual consent. The subscribers have withdrawn from the concern and sold out their interest to A. M. Wallingford and Geo. H. Taylor, who are alone authorized to settle the business of the house. In retiring from the business, we would ask for our successors continuance oft that patronage so liberally extended to us. W. M. Calvert, Jas. N. Morrison.

The Maysville Eagle

Turnpike Road Notice. The stockholders in the Maysville and Mount Sterling Turnpike Road, are hereby notified, that a call of ten dollars on each share of stock in said road is required to be paid on the 16th day of November next; and that ten dollars on the share is required to be paid every sixty days thereafter until the whole amount subscribed shall be paid in. John A. Cavan, Pres't. Flemingsburg, Oct. 25, 1837

Removal of Head Quarters. Henry B. Cummins, Respectfully reminds his friends and the public, that the Head Quarters Eating House, has been removed to an eligible and spacious house on Front street, recently occupied by Messrs. McCardle and Ryan, where those who wish to sip good beverages and feast upon the luxuries of the season, are requested to give him a call. As heretofore, his best exertions will be given to satisfy his customers, and no pains will be spared to render the establishment creditable to the city. Nov. 2, 1837.

Beatty's Rifle Powder. January & Huston.

Spanish Sigars. 12 thousand just received and for sale by J. W. Johnston & Co. Druggist.

New Books at the Eagle Book Store.

R.G. Dobyns & Co. have on hand a large and well selected assortment of Summer and Fall goods, which they offer very low for cash, or on liberal credit. Persons wishing to purchase, would find it much to their advantage to give them a call. Maysville, July 26, 1837

F.T. Chambers, Counselor & Attorney at Law, Washington, Ky. Will practice in the Mason, Fleming, Bracken and Nicholas Courts. Office on the public square in F? Row. Washington, Nov 22, 1837

New Goods. Morton, Proctor & Co. Are now opening a large and general assortment of Staple and Fancy Goods, suitable for the present and approaching season, all of which have been selected with great care in the cities of Baltimore, Philadelphia and New York, and will be sold on the most reasonable terms, by wholesale or retail. They invite their friends and the public to give them an early call. Maysville, September 27, 1837.

Window Glass. For sale by Clarke & Ryan. February 25, 1837

The Maysville Eagle

Henry Waller, Attorney at Law, Maysville, Ky. Office on Sutton Street, nearly opposite Mrs. Goddard's old stand. Feb. 2, 1837

Cash for Wheat. We will give 80 cents cash per bushel for all good merchantable wheat delivered at our Steam Mill in Maysville, in all the month of November. Cleaney & Shultz. Nov. 8, 1837

Books for sale E. Cox, Front Street, Maysville, Nov. 15, 1837.

$100 Reward. Strayed or stolen from the subscriber living three miles west of Poplar Plains, in Fleming County, on the night of the 6th of October, a bay horse and dark brown mare. The horse was 4 years old in the spring, about 15 ½ hands high, light mane, four white feet, tolerably well made, and paces well. The mare is of a dark brown color, four years old last spring, full 16 hands high, one of the hind feet white, has a scar from a cut on her left ham string, high forehead - no brands or other marks recollected, I will give the above reward for the thief and horses, if the were stolen or $20 for the two horses - or $10 for either, if delivered to me as above. Thomas F. Richardson. Fleming County, Nov. 1, 1837

Eagle Tavern, corner of Front and Market Streets, Maysville, Ky. Mrs. Judith Goddard, (late of the Washington Hotel) Having been compelled to give up the house she has so long occupied takes pleasure in informing her friends and the traveling public, that she has succeeded in getting that old established house, known as the Eagle Tavern, (formerly in the occupancy of John T. Langhorne, and more recently kept by John Dudley), where she will at all times be pleased to see her old friends and others who may be disposed to favor her with their custom. In taking leave of the stand she has so long occupied, she would be doing injustice to her own feelings were she not to return her grateful acknowledgments to those who have so kindly supported her for the last four years, and in asking a continuance of the favors which has been invariably extended to her, she pledges herself that no exertion shall be wanting on her part to merit it. For the management of her present establishment she makes no pr promise, but referring to her past, ventures to name all who may visit her house that no pains or expense shall be spared to render their stay at once comfortable and agreeable. Her table will as usual present every delicacy the market affords, and her bar will be supplied with the choicest wines and liquors. Maysville, October 18, 1837.

Strayed from the subscriber, living in Maysville, Ky. About the 20th of November last, a small light brindle cow. Any person delivering said cow

The Maysville Eagle

to me, in Maysville, or giving information so that I get her, shall be reasonably rewarded. Thomas S. Thornley. Maysville, October 28, 1837.

Nails for sale. Gaylord & Co.

Sash. Just received by Parker & Sharp

Dr. W. H. Robertson, Tenders his services in the various branches of his profession, to the citizens of Minerva and adjacent country. His office is on Wm.P. Thomas' lot, nearly opposite Mrs. Craig's. May 14th 1835.

Lamps, China, Glass and Fancy Goods. At No. 203 Main Street, between 5th and 6th. Nathan Sampson, Cincinnati, July 8, 1837

Patent Coffee Mills. J. B. M'Ilvain. Maysville, July 8, 1837.

Covington Cotton Yarns. R. Buchanan. Cincinnati, Sept. 9, 1837

Removal. P. Carpenter, would inform his friends, and the public generally, that he has removed his shop a few doors east of his old stand, and one door to the right of Coburn & Stockwell's Store, where he is now opening a general assortment of boots and shoes, much larger than usual, His stock having been selected by him with much care and attention of every description and of the neatest fashion. P. Carpenter returns his sincere thanks to a generous and discrimination public, for their liberal patronage, and hopes by punctual attention, and good bargains to merit a continuance. Maysville, Feb. 15, 1837

Plough Factory and Foundry, Lewis, Benjam (sic) N. and James Jacobs, successors J & L. Jacobs, under the firm Lewis Jacobs & Co. Will continue to carry on the plough factory and foundry at the old stand on Third Street. They will keep constantly on hand a large quantity and superior quality of the improved patent ploughs and mould boards, which will be made of the very best materials, and the workmanship warranted equal to any manufactured in the country. They solicit a continuance of the extensive patronage which they have enjoyed for years past. Maysville, Sept. 10, 1836

Fresh Drugs. William R. Wood has just received at his drug store, corner of Front and Main Cross Streets, a large and extensive assortment of drugs, medicines & paints, which he will sell at moderate prices for cash, or on credit to approved customers. Maysville, May 13.

The Maysville Eagle

Falling of the Womb, cured by external application. Dr. A.G. Hull's utero abdominal supporter. Amos G. Hull A large assortment just received by J. W. Johnston, Druggist. Sept 2, 1837.

Notice. All those indebted to the subscriber, either by Note or Book account are earnestly requested to call and pay the same without delay. E. Tureman. May 31, 1837.

Law Notice. The partnership heretofore existing between M'Clung and Taylor, having been dissolved by limitation, John A. M'Clung will henceforth practice law in the counties of Mason, Lewis, Fleming and Greenup. His office is that recently occupied by John Chambers, Esq. Washington, Sept. 13, 1837.

New Wholesale Tin & Sheet Iron Manufactory. Nathan Davis, respectfully informs his friends and the public, that he continues the above business in the three story brick building lately occupied by Messrs. Cutter and Jackson, as a wholesale Grocery and Liquor Store, on Sutton Street, opposite the Eagle Book Store and Printing Office, where he intends keeping constantly on hand, a very large and general assortment of Tin and sheet iron ware of every description, which he is determined to sell at reduced prices. Merchants and dealers in the above articles are particularly invited to call and examine his stock as he warrants it to be made of the best materials, and altogether a new and superior style to any offered in this market. He also keeps on hand, the improved double reflecting portable oven, of various sizes, for baking and roasting meat and bread, which he will sell 25 per cent of upwards below the former prices. He also keeps on hand house work of every description in the Tinning Business, such as house heads, guttering, conducting pipe and valley tin. Nathan Davis also continues to manufacture stone ware, and has on hand 3,000 gallons, and intends keeping a large assortment on hand, next door above their tin ware store. Maysville, October 14, 1837.

Vegetable Medicines. Dr. G. Dunbar. Having permanently located in the city of Maysville, respectfully informs the citizens of the place and its vicinity, that he will continue the practice of Medicine, Surgery & c. Dr. Dunbar is a graduate of the Reformed Medical College of Worthington Ohio. There a system of practice..... to that taught in other Colleges, or pursued by other physicians; the remedial agents being derived from the vegetable kingdom, which are more congenial to the human frame, less dangerous, and at the same time more efficacious than the strong mineral

The Maysville Eagle

medicines or poisons - not entailing on the constitution any subsequent bad effects. The efficacy of this practice has been proved, for more than half a century, combining the improvements of the most distinguished medical men of the present or any other age - Its superiority has been so repeatedly demonstrated, as to satisfy the most wavering and skeptical. It has been tested in every variety and form of disease; and its salutary effects witnessed where the mercurial or mineral treatment has been pursued without any beneficial effect, but to the great injury of the constitution. The treatment is so much at variance with that of other physicians that their opposition, calumny & c. are considerable; but their ignorance of the practice offers some excuse or apology for their conduct towards it. Having studied the modern fashionable or mineral practice, in addition to the botanical and having closely observed the effects of both, he hesitates not to say that the practice of giving mercury and other poisonous minerals, will no longer exist, when people learn the difference between the two kinds of treatment. Think not that this system advocates ignorance or the unity of disease; nor does it have any connection with such as are called "root or Indian doctors, patent or steam doctors, herbalists, empiricks & c. Though some of these are very successful in the treatment of many diseases; because they avail themselves of the resources afforded by active plants, often neglected or unknown to the regular practitioners. Office on Main Cross Street, east side, first door above Second St. May 10, 1837.

Saddling. The undersigned would respectfully inform the public and his friends, in general, that he has commenced the above business in the town of Washington, in the shop opposite Dr. Rannells' shop, in all its various branches. All kinds of saddles bridles and harnesses (both carriage and wagon) made on the shortest notice. William Lokey. July 15, 1837

Livery Stable. Hawkins Hand, and Evan T. Burgoyne, Respectfully inform their friends and the public, that they have become proprietors of the livery stable, formerly occupied by Mr. Nathan Heath, on Second , not far from Main Cross or Market Street. They assure those who may confide horses to their care, that they will keep them as cheap, and pay as much attention to them as any establishment in the place. Mr. H's long experience in purchasing provender, furnishes a sure guaranty that they will at all times be supplied with the best of that indispensable requisite in keeping a good table. Horses & c. for hire at fair prices. January 21, 1837

Wm. R. Beatty and C.S. Rannells. Have entered into co-partnership in the practice of law in Mason. They will give their united attention to all

The Maysville Eagle

business entrusted to them. Their office in Washington fronting the public square, the same formerly occupied by Judge Reid. Nov. 30, 1836

R. J. Langhorne, would inform his friends and old customers, that he has sold and disposed of his stock in trade, to William & Nathan Poyntz, who will conduct the business at his old stand, and he asks for the new house, the liberal patronage he has always enjoyed. He has also handed over to them the goods consigned as commissions. R. J. Langhorne. February 18, 1837. William & Nat. Poyntz, Would respectfully inform the old customers of the house of R. J. Langhorne, in the commission business, in the city of Maysville. They respectfully request a continuance of their business and would be grateful to the public generally for a liberal share of patronage. Wm. & Nat. Poyntz. February 18, 1837

The debtors of R. J. Langhorne, are informed that their notes and accounts, will be found in the hands of A. Berry, whom I have engaged as a clerk, to close the same- Mr. Berry will be found at the late office of R. J. Langhorne, or will wait on the various debtors with their notes or accounts for liquidation. Thomas Y. Payne. February 25, 1837

$50 Reward. Ranaway from the subscriber, 6 miles from Lexington, on the old Limestone Road, on Wednesday, 1st inst., A Negro Man, Named Henry, about 53 years of age, 5 feet 10 or 11 inches high,, very bald, with whiskers somewhat grey, large white eyes and large nose; and is apt to stammer a little when frightened. He had on when he went off, a dress coat and pantaloons of a reddish brown jeans, and a black fur hat, which he may change to avoid detection. He has probably made for the state of Ohio, as he has done so on two former occasions, on one of which he was apprehended and brought back. I will give the above reward of Fifty Dollars, for the apprehension of said slave, and his confinement in any jail so that I get him again, if taken out of state – twenty-five, if taken in any of the remote counties of this state fifteen, if taken in any county adjoining Fayette- ten if taken in Fayette County. John Rogers. Fayette Co. Nov 10, 1837

The New Court House in Lewis County, Notice to Carpenters & c. Archibald Frizzel, John P. Savage, Augustine C. Owens, Benjamin Given, Jacob Myers, James Redden, Sr. , Joseph Robb, Comm'rs. Clarksburg, Nov 4, 1837

$200 Reward. Ranaway from the subscriber, at Maysville, K., on Saturday night, the 21st inst., A Negro Boy, Named Nelson, as he is sometimes

The Maysville Eagle

called. He is about 19 or 20 years old, 5 feet 9 or 10 inches high, of slender form, dark copper complexion and small head. He has large flat feet which he turns out a good deal in walking, and has a swing in his gait, which when he is fatigued amounts to almost lameness, owing to a weakness of his ankles. He has long arms, is rather quick spoken and has a pleasant countenance while speaking. He had on when he left home a brown cloth frock coat, white muslin shirt, coarse heavy shoes (high) almost new. His other clothing not recollected. It is thought from some circumstances which have come to my knowledge, that he will endeavor to strike the Ohio Canal near to Portsmouth, Ohio, and follow it through Ohio in his way to the Lakes. I will give the above reward for him if taken out of the State of Kentucky and delivered to J. S. or W. Chambers, Maysville, Ky. Or secured in any jail in this state so that I can get him or fifty dollars if taken in the state of Kentucky. Wm. B. Phillips. Oct 25, 1837

Fresh Drugs just received J.W., Johnson Druggist

Copper, Tin & Sheet Iron Ware. John C. Reid respectfully informs his friends and the public, that he continues to manufacture at his old stand, corner of Main Cross and 2nd streets, a short distance below the Market House, towards the river, all the various articles in his line of business, and where he keeps constantly on hand a large assortment of ware of the best quality, and on terms as accommodating as they can be bought in that city, or elsewhere, without any exception. His long and well tried experience in business, together with a number of experienced workmen in his employ, will enable him to execute all orders with neatness and dispatch, and he pledges himself that his work shall not be excelled in quality of material, workmanship, or cheapness. Merchants and all others wishing to purchase, are invited to call and see for themselves. Cooking, coal and wood stoves and common grates all sizes are constantly kept on hand for sale. Maysville, Jan. 4, 1837

Mr. Thomas Bragg, Take notice, that upon the 11th day of January, 1838, at the office of William R. Beatty in Greenupsburg, I will take the depositions of John Morton and others, and at the house of Mrs. Letitia Morton in Greenup county, on the 12th day of January 1838, I will take the deposition of the said Letitia Morton and others, all to be used on the trial of the suit in chancery, now pending in the Greenup Circuit Court, in which I am complainant and yourself, and others defendants. John Brown, Nov. 15, 1837

The Maysville Eagle

Messrs. A. Hoage, William Stewart, Robert C. Green and C. P. Wetmore, you will take notice, that upon the 11th day of January 1838, at the office of William R. Beatty in the town of Greenupsburg, the depositions of Lewis D. Ross, R.A. Dayton and others will be taken to be used on the trial of the five suits in chancery, now pending in the Greenup Circuit Court, in all of which you are defendants and in the first of which William Snidow is complainant, William I Poage in the second, George Hart in the third, Wade Hampton in the fourth, and John Lavender in the fifth. Should any thing prevent the taking of the depositions on the day named they will be taken at the same place on the 13th day of January 1838. W. R. Beatty, A. H. Frizzel, Attorneys. November 15, 1837

Messrs. Randall Hutchinson and Israel P. Hutchison, take notice, that in New Ark, in the state of New Jersey, at the office of the Mayor of said place upon the 8th day of February 1838, I will take the deposition of Mathew H. Henderson, to be used as evidence on the trial of the suit in Chancery, now pending in the Greenup Circuit Court, wherein I am complainant, and yourself and others defendants. William H. Harrison. September 15, 1837

Mr. Wm. C. Sloan, Take notice that upon the 11th day of January, 1838, at the court house in Greenupsburg, I will take the depositions of Isaac G. Dysart, and Melvina Howe, to be used as evidence on the trial of the suit in chancery, now pending in the Greenup Circuit Court, in which I am complainant, and yourself and others defendants. Elizabeth Howe, November 15, 1837

Taken up as a stray by John A. Keith, living in Charleston Bottom, three miles below Maysville, Mason County, A small bay mare, about fourteen and a half hands high, supposed to be five years old next spring, having collar marks on the neck, a sore on the back, a saddle spot on the right side of the back, a few white hairs in the forehead, left hind foot white, and shod all round; appraised to $30 by Rodney Sullivan and Reason Wherney before me this 23rd September, 1837 M. Markland, J. P. November 15, 1837

Insurance Office. Protection. Having been appointed for the Protectior Insurance Company at Hartford, in place of Mr. John B. Gibson, their late agent; I am now prepared to take risks on stores, dwelling houses, barns, factory's Mills & c. and on cargoes of steam, keep or flat boats, on as moderate forms as any office in the west, and the promptness in which the office has heretofore met and paid all losses either by land or water, will, I

The Maysville Eagle

hope, be a guarantee for a liberal support. The different losses that have been paid in the west, in the last four years, has been upwards of $160,000. Please apply at my counting room for policies. All letters addressed to me on the subject of insurance will be promptly attended to Jno. B. McIvain, agt. Maysville, Oct 8, 1838

Maysville Insurance Company, continue to make insurance on goods, wares, merchandise and produce of every description, against lose or damage by fire. Also on the cargoes of steam, keel, or flat boats on any of the rivers, lakes, bayous, or canals, or from any one port in the United States to another. They also make insurance on lives, grant annuities and make any contracts in which the casualties of life are principally involved. Wm. Mackey, President, Christian Shultz, William Huston, Ric'd Henry Lee, Richard Collins, James N. Morrison, Edward Cox, Directors, Matthew Markland, Secretary, January 1837

Lumber. Morris A. Hutchins, Takes this method of conveying to his friends and former customers, his sincere thanks for the very liberal patronage which has been extended to him heretofore, having by dint of perseverance been enabled to supply himself with a large assortment of the above named article, comprising an assortment of every description and almost that is landed at Maysville..... His lumber is on Third Street, directly opposite Mr. H. Hand's Wagon Yard, where he will generally be found, or at his dwelling, on the corner of Limestone and Third Streets. Maysville, July 27, 1836

Hogs! Hogs! Hogs! The pork house and slaughtering establishment lately in the occupancy of Messrs. Hand and Dodson has been purchased by the undersigned, and is now undergoing repairs and improvements, by means of which they will be able to render satisfaction to their patrons, to effect which purpose no pains will be spared. Marshall Curtis & Co. P. S. Lard Kegs, Pork Barrels and Salt can be procured in Maysville. Sept. 13, 1837

August 14, 1841

The Maysville Eagle, is printed and published semi-weekly, (Wednesday and Saturdays) By Lewis Collins, at five dollars, payable semi-annually or four dollars in advance.

There is a spirit of exquisite tenderness and delicacy about the following lines from the pen of Mrs. Norton, which commends them at once to the mind of the reader. The spirit they breathe, is soft and melancholy, like the

The Maysville Eagle

last taint sigh which the evening zephyr calls forth from the AEalean harp. It is an appeal which makes its way directly to the heart. We have been friends together and Heaven two poems by Mrs. Norton, published in full, a couple of lines are unreadable.

A call, we contemplate starting East about the 15th August to make our fall purchases. We would be glad if our customers would call and settle up by that time. W. Lashbrooke & Sons. Washington, July 17, 41

Cavindish Tobacco. W & N. Poyntz

Sugar for sale by G. M. Procter

Dried Peaches for sale by H. P. Peers,

Old Bourbon, A. M. January & Son.

Window Glass Leach & Dobyns.

Gillott's Pens for sale at E. Cox's Bookstore.

Negro Boy for sale, A likely Negro Boy is offered for sale. Inquire of John S. Wells or Granville ?, Orangeburg, Mason Co, Ky.

Hardware House, L. Collins having purchased interest of B. B. Reynolds in the hardware house, in Maysville, and become an equal partner in said establishment, the business will hereafter be permanently continued at the old stand under the firm of N. D. Hunter & Co. Maysville, June 30th, 1841

60 sacks superior Rio Coffee for sale by Geo M. Procter.
Pumps for Hemp Rotters. W. & Nat. Poyntz
Vinegar, Leach & Dobyns
Rio Coffee A. M. January & Son
Cider Vinegar. H. P. Peers, corner of Market and Second Maysville
Collins' Axes, Jno B. Mclvain

To Journeymen potters, Thomas & Mendell, at their pottery immediately below the city of Maysville, will give constant employment and good wages, to four or five journeymen potters, with good moral character and industrious habits. April 17

The Maysville Eagle

Confidence Restored. A lot of the very best quality of Deboree Cigars, on hand and for sale by Hugh McCullough, Maysville March 6

Town Lot for sale. I will sell at private sale, on good terms one half of the vacant lot lying between Dan'l Spalding and the Seminary lot in this city. R. C. Weirick for Henry Weirick, Maysville, May 5, 1841

Coffee Sugar Raisins & c for sale by Henry Cutter & Co.

Law Notice. W.R. Beatty, of Greenupsburg, and M Markland of Maysville, attorneys at Law, have associated themselves in practice, in the Mason Circuit Court. Business confided to them, will receive their joint and prompt attention. Office on Main-cross Street, Maysville, formerly occupied by M. Markland. June 19, '41

Tho. Y. Payne & H. Waler, Attorneys at Law, Maysville, Ky. Will practice law in partnership in the courts of Mason, Bracken, Fleming, Nicholas, Lewis and Greenup, and in the court of Appeals. Office on Front Street, three doors above Dr. Seaton's shop. Maysville, June 19, 1841

Fresh Corn & Rye Meal, kept constantly on hand and for sale. Also, Chopped rye and crushed corn, for horse and cow feed. Mill adjoining the livery stable, Second Street. Culbertson & Weedon, July 14th '41

Dry Goods at Wholesale. The undersigned have upon hand, a good stock of dry goods to which they invite the attention of country merchants. Stand upon Market Street, the same that was occupied by Pearce, Fant and Brodrick. L. C. & H. P. Pearce. Maysville 24th July, '41

J. A. M'Clung & H. Taylor Attorneys At Law, Washington, Ky. Will hereafter practice law in partnership in the Mason Circuit.

Dr. Nelson, Continues the practice of Physic, Washington. His office is the same recently occupied by Nelson Marshall. Washington, July 25, 1840

F. T. Hord & J. R. Reid. Have associated themselves in the practice of the law in Mason County, and will attend to all business confided to them. Mayville, July 24, 1839

L. J. Procter, Counselor and Attorney at Law, Maysville Ky. Will make collections and remit to order. His office is on Main Cross Street No. 6 one door above the office of Maysville Insurance Company. Nov 23, 1839

The Maysville Eagle

For sale a likely female servant about 18 years of age, brought up entirely to house work. Inquire of the Editor. April 17, 1841

Card. Maxwell & Buchanan, commission & Forwarding Merchants, No. 65 Camp Street New Orleans. Refer to Messrs A. M. January & Son, Maysville, Jno. B. McIlvaine, Esq. Robert S. Todd, Esq. Lexington. Andrew & Robert Buchanan Louisville, Robert Buchanan Esq. Cincinnati. April 28, 1841

Cash Wanted. No mistake, I want money. All persons knowing themselves indebted for goods or drugs would confer and everlasting favor by calling and paying up their accounts and notes, as it is very disagreeable to dun every day. I am compelled to meet my liabilities, and must of course ask my customers to be up and doing the same the law is a bad article to wait for. A fine stack of Goods & Drugs for sale extremely low for cash – come and try J. W. Johnston. Maysville, May 8, 41

Dissolution of Partnership. The partnership heretofore existing under the firm of Pearce, Fant & Brodrick, in the sale of dry goods, has this day been dissolved by mutual consent. Mr. Lewis C. Pearce, having purchased the entire interest of R. C. Fant & J. F. Brodrick, in the late firm. The notes and accounts will remain at the old stand, where one of the late firm, will at all times be found, to make such settlements as will be necessary to close the business of the house. We hope, those who know their accounts or notes to be due, will make immediate payment. H. P. Pearce, R. C. Fant, J. F.. Brodrick. Maysville, 24, July 1841

A superior article of family flour on hand and for sale by G. M. Procter, April 7, 1841.

For sale, a likely female servant and her children; the mother is about 25 years of age, the boy is 1 year and 7 months and the girl 7 months of age. The woman is of good steady habits and capable of doing house work, such as cooking, washing & c. Enquire of the Editor of the Eagle.

For sale, a female servant girl, a good washer and ironer, and capable house servant, aged about 21 years. Enquire at the Eagle Book Store. May 22

For sale, A Negro Woman under middle age, well skilled in household and kitchen duties, with two young children. Apply at this office, or to Jno. S. Forman. June 16

Scrofula or Kings Evil. From the Flemingburg Kentuckian. Mr. Chapman – Permit me through the columns of your paper to inform the public of a case of Scrofula or King's evil, cured by Dr. Robertson of Flemingsburgh. A boy of mine was afflicted with scrofula for two years. He was attended by a respectable physician for twelve months, during which time he went blind. Dr. Robertson was called to see him on the first of May; he had then been blind nine months, his face was very much swollen, his head was very sore, his eyes, ears, nose, neck and many places about his face were running sores, and his body and extremities swollen. In about six weeks he opened his eyes. He is now perfectly well, and you could not tell that he had been diseased were in not for some scars about his neck. I write the above, hoping many may profit by it. Yours with great respect. John H. Evans. Fleming Co. Nov 2, '40

Fruit Trees. The subscriber begs leave to inform those who wish to supply themselves with good Apple trees, to give him a call, as he has a large quantity and great variety of as good Apple trees as can be found in any section of country. Thomas H. Williams. Washington, Ky. March 10

Tanners Oil. A few barrels best tanners oil, just received and for sale on consignment. Also, 5 gro. Nerve and bone liniment by Doct. A. Seaton, May 29, '41

Drugs! Drugs! Drugs! Not selling in any way, just at this particular time – but for sale at a fair profit, or cost and carriage to the needful – punctual customers on liberal time. Friends or not, call at No. 10, Market Street, you can be served by J. W. Johnston, Druggist, July 20 '41

Specimen of Female industry – We were shown yesterday (says the Georgia Messenger,) five beautiful silk shawls, made of doubled and twisted sewing silk.... We take pride in the fact they were made by a native of Georgia. They are the handiwork of Mrs. Oliver W. Cox, of Henry County, Georgia who raised the worms, reeled and twisted the silk, and knotted the shawls. She is a pattern of female skill and industry to her sex, which if generally imitated, will be the means of making the fair of Georgia useful as they are attentive, and helpmates in every deed...

Maysville Eagle, Saturday, August 14, 1841

The Maysville Eagle

Married on Tuesday the 4th instant, at Hamilton, Ohio, Mr. J. Smith McKenny, Printer, of Burlington, Iowa Territory to Miss Susan E. daughter of Judge Jas. O'Conner.

Deaths. At Cabell's Dale, the family seat, in Fayette County, on the afternoon of Wednesday the 4th instant, after a lingering illness, having just completed his 44th year, the Rev. Dr. John Breckenridge, son of the late Hon. John Breckenridge, and for the last twenty years known throughout the U. S. as a most laborious minister of the gospel of God.

In Frankfort, on the 4th instant, Churchill Samuel, Esq. President of the Branch Bank of Kentucky in that place.

Steam Feather Renovator. The subscriber would respectfully inform his fellow citizens that he has resumed for a short time the business of renovating feathers, in the house formerly kept as a grocery store, on the lower grade and next door below George Collins & Co's China Store. The work is done entirely by steam, no fire going near the feathers and no possibility of scorching or otherwise injuring them..... price 5 cents per pound. John Burrows. August 14th 1841. The undersigned most cheerfully state, that they have had their beds renovated by Mr. John Burrow, and with decided benefit to the feathers; the process restoring to them their original softness and elasticity. They would further recommend the process as being lightly conducive to health, from its effect in correcting any tendency to putrescence in new, and removing all fetid, offensive, or unwholesome odors from old feathers. Jno. Shacklefold, Jno. M. Duke, Mrs. E. B. Langhorne, A.C. Respess, J. C. Coleman, Geo. Herbst, E. Cox, John C. Reed, T. M. Donovan, Wm.M. Poyntz, P. B. Jones, M. Markland.

Madame Barabino, French Embroderies, laces and hosiery from Paris. Madame B. begs leave to inform the ladies of this vicinity, that she will open an extensive assortment of the above mentioned articles of the richest quality, which she offers at the lowest prices, at the house of William Mackey, Front Street, No. 2, next door to York and Co's Lottery Office. Ladies desirous of purchasing will do her the honor of calling and satisfying themselves, as to style and quality. Maysville, Aug. 14, '41

Dissolution. The partnership heretofore existing between Thos. W. Baltzell and E. Johnson, expired on the 26th of July last, and the business of said firm will be closed by Thos. W. Baltzell. Notice. Thos. W. Baltzell having taken Jonas Eddy and James Baltzell in company with him, the mercantile business will still be conducted by them under the firm of Baltzell, Eddy & Co. Mayslick, Aug. 14 '41

Mason Patroll. The Mason County Patroll met on Monday the 12th of July, 1841, in the clerk's office. Present, Peter Driskell, Baldwin Harl, William Soward, Charles S. Mitchell, Thomas Glasscock, and James Lynn, and elected Peter Driskell, Captain. And the said Captain forthwith appointed the following officers to wit. First Lieutenant, Baldwin Harl, Second, A. A. Wadsworth, Third, Thomas Glasscock, Respectfully submitted to the county court of Mason County, Peter Driskell, Aug 11 41

A Pocket book found. The undersigned picked up a pocket book, on the 22nd day of June last, about one mile and a fourth south of Washington, Mason County, on the turnpike road, containing some money and papers, which the owner can have by describing and paying for this notice. John P. Metcalfe. Fleming Co. Ky. Aug 11, '41

$200 Reward. Ranaway from the subscriber a Negro boy named John. He is about 5 feet 6 inches high and a likely boy, with open fine countenance. He has been working with me for about four years at the painting business. He is about 19 years of age. His upper most teeth are rather far apart and very white. I will give the above reward if he is taken out of the state. $100 if taken in any of the counties bordering on the Ohio River; $50 if taken in any of the middle counties, and $30 if taken in Fayette or any of the adjoining counties, and lodged in jail, and notice sent to Athens, Fayette County, Kentucky. Alfred Cohen

Rev. I Covert's Balm of life: A new and valuable remedy for the cure of Consumption, Asthma, Bronchitis, Croup, Whooping Cough, and all diseases of the lungs and Windpipe. For sale by Dr. A. Seaton, Maysville.

Selling off at Cost. Unable to attend to business, I wish to dispose of my stock of goods, a good assortment for a retail house, mostly of late importation and some of the present. I will take all kinds of produce. Terms, under five dollars cash, over five and under one hundred dollars, six months credit, over one hundred dollars, twelve months credit; approved notes will be required. I will also sell town property and a small farm of one hundred and sixty acres, joining the town of Eaton, Preble County, Ohio; I will take State Bonds at par for the above property. I hope my old customers have not forgotten their notes and accounts not paid, and in order to facilitate payment, I will take all kinds of young stock that my

The Maysville Eagle

overseer and manager, John S. Vimont, will approve of; apply to him on the farm, or in Millersburg, where he will be found at all times. Lewis Vimont. Millersburg, April 7th, 1841

An ordinance to establish a common school in the city of Maysville. .... And the said school shall be free for all children over the age of seven and under seventeen years of age, whose parents, masters or guardians reside within the city of Maysville. Nat. Poyntz, pres pro tem, M. Markland, City Clerk. August 7 '41

Administrator's Sale. 150 barrels of old bourbon whiskey, will be offered for sale, on credit until Christmas. Notes with approved endorsements will be required payable in Bank. The whiskey will be offered for sale in front of the warehouses of Jno. B. McIivain and Artus & Metcalfe, on the first Monday in September next, being the 6th day of the month. John Williams, Adm'r. of the estate of Sam'l Williams, dec'd. Maysville.

Sign of the Big Boot. V. Dewein, respectfully informs his customers and the public in general that he is prepared to manufacture boots and shoes of all descriptions, at as low a rate as can be done elsewhere. I would inform those wishing any work made to order, that they can be accommodated on a short notice, as I am determined to spare no pains, or labor to please those that may favor me with a call. A good assortment of custom made boots and shoes, constantly kept on hand. Also a first rate article of clack and colored kid slippers, which I will sell low for cash or on a short credit to those that pay punctually. Maysville, August 7, '41

Mason Agricultural Society. A. Beatty, President M. A. S. August 7, '41

Stray Cow. Strayed away from the subscriber about the middle of June, a large pale red cow, fine form – I think she has a crop off her left ear, and gimblet holes in both of her horns. I will remunerate any one for their trouble, if they will deliver her in Maysville, or any information respecting her will be thankfully received if left at the Eagle office, or with Mr. H. P. Peers. W. W. Robb. Aug 4'41

State of Kentucky, Nicholas Circuit, Sct. July Term 1841. Ann Mayhugh's adm'r against Ann Mayhugh's Heirs & C. in Chancery. This cause having been refered to the Master Commissioner, ?asertain and report .. unreadable. All persons having claims against said estate, are hereby required to prove them before me, on or before the 3rd Monday in October

The Maysville Eagle
next, at my office, in the town of Carlisle, where I can at all times be found. L. Marston, Master Commissioner.

Notice, the partnership of W. V. Morris & Co was dissolved in October last. It is therefore absolutely necessary to collect all claims due said concern. Payment must be made without delay to W. V. Morris and B. E. Walder, of Mayslick, or J. P. Dobyns, Maysville.

On or about the 15th of August next we expect to go East for our fall and winter supply of goods and will be thankful to our customers for all the assistance they can render us. We have some notes and accounts of long standing, which we expect to be cashed before our departure. Taylor & Green. Washington, July 14th 1841

Notice. The partnership heretofore existing between B. B. Reynolds and N. D. Hunter, under the firm of Reynolds & Hunter, in the hardware business is this day dissolved by mutual consent. All debts due said firm are by contract, to be paid to N. D. Hunter & Co., their successors in business. B. B. Reynolds, N. D. Hunter, Maysville, June 25, 1841

$100 Reward. Ranaway from the subscriber, living in Fleming County, Ky. On Sunday night the 25th instant a Negro man named Pompey. A dark mulatto or copper color, with a nappy head, full face, stout and well built, weight from 165 to 170 lbs; 24 years old, 5 feet 7 inches high, very ingenious and fond of talk, and quite pleasant in his manners; has a good set of fore-teeth, but has recently lost several of his jaw teeth, a remarkable scar on the lower part of the palm of one of his hands believed to be the right, produced from the cut of a scythe last year. Had on when he went away, a pair of blue cloth pantaloons, a striped velvet waistcoat, black fur or silk hat. His other clothing not recollected. He has no doubt a free pass, obtained from some scoundrel in the neighborhood. The above reward will be given for his apprehension out of the state or fifty dollars if taken out of the counties of Fleming, Mason or Lewis, or twenty five dollars if taken in either county named and all reasonable expenses, if delivered to me in Fleming County, or secured in any jail so that I can get him again. William Farrow, Sen'r. Fleming County, North Fork of Licking, 12 miles S. E. of Maysville. July 28, 1841

Stray Horse. Strayed from the pasture of Wm E. Wilson, near Mayslick, about the 20th of June, a blood bay ball faced horse, believed to have two white feet. Any person giving information or delivering said horse to the

The Maysville Eagle

undersigned will be liberally rewarded. E.P. Johnston & Co. Per M. Stanley, agent Maysville, July 7, '41

Kentucky State Lottery. For the benefit of the Grand Lodge of Ky. Tickets $5 halves $2.50 for sale by D. Carrell

Literature Lottery, authorized by the state of Kentucky for the benefit of Shelby College Draws at Covington, Ky, every day (Sundays excepted) Lucky Office of A. F. Yorke & Co. Corner of Front and Market Streets, Aug. 4, Maysville

Saddle & Harness manufactory. The subscriber respectfully informs his friends and the public, that he has commenced the above business in the village of Minerva; where he will keep on hand a general assortment of saddles, bridles martingales, harnesses & c. manufactured from the best of materials and by experienced workmen. He will sell any of the above articles on as reasonable terms as they can be purchased elsewhere. From his long experience in the business he respects to receive a share of the public patronage. Wm O. Fant. Minerva, July 31, '41

Notice. At the lower end of Maysville, corner of Second and Short streets the subscriber will contract to build machinery or repair all kinds now in use in this section of country – having a general knowledge of machinery and a practical operator for twenty years, he flatters himself that he will be able to give general satisfaction to all those who may please to patronize him. Patterns furnished and gearing filled to order; he will promptly attend to the procuring of all kinds of castings, suitable to the business they are designed for – mill spindles and other iron turning down at short notice, taps and dyes for screw cutting, and all other small work appertaining to machinery , warranted not inferior to any done elsewhere. A reasonable price for materials and necessary work will be charged except there be unnecessary work ordered. Likewise the subscriber will attend in person to the repairing of machinery, that cannot conveniently be sent to Maysville. Samuel McCauley. July 28, '41

To Country Merchants. W & C. Fellowes & Co., Corner of Main and Wall Streets, Louisville, Ky. Would respectfully inform country merchants, that they will offer purchasers the ensuing fall, one of the largest stock of dry goods ever opened west of the mountains, and from the fact that they make all their purchases from the first hands, and at as low prices as any Eastern jobber, they believe they can sell their goods at Eastern jobbing prices, with a fair allowance for exchange, charges, interest & c. Their terms are cash,

The Maysville Eagle

or six months to punctual men, and they solicit from all such a visit and examination. Their stock will be completed by the 15th of September. July 28, '41

Notice!!! All persons knowing themselves indebted to the subscribers will please call and settle, on or previous to the 10th August next; as longer indulgence cannot be given. S. L. Blaine & Co. July 21, '41

Dr. A. M. McKinney, respectfully tenders his professional services to the citizens of Murphysville and its vicinity, in the practice of medicine, surgery and midwifery. July 17, '41

Boards & Shingles, G. Sibbald Aberdeen, Ohio June 26, '41

Doct. A. G. Burgess, Will continue the practice of Medicine in Mayslick and surrounding country. His office is the one formerly occupied by Doctor Tebbs. Mayslick, June 30 '41

$150 Reward. Ranaway from the subscriber, living in Mason county, near Orangeburg, on Saturday evening the 19th inst. A Negro boy by the name of Aaron, but is generally called Kelly, very black, with light beard, 23 years of age, 5 feet 6 inches high, weighs about 170 lbs. Had on when he left, a black fur hat, pretty well made, tow linen pantaloons, and dark roundabouts – having other clothing with him it is likely he may have changed his dress. The above reward will be given for said boy if taken out of state & lodged in jail that I may get him. $75 if taken out of the county, or $25 if taken in the county of Mason. Granville H. Dye. June 23, 1841

Public Sale of Real and Personal Estate. The undersigned wishing to remove to Illinois will sell his entire landed estate, which is located adjacent to the town of Powersville, in Bracken County, Ky. Embracing that well known tavern stand in said town, and a number of houses and lots, which are well adapted to a family. Also a tan-yard interest and about 150 acres of land all adjoining said town. Also a farm, lying about 3 miles southwest of said town and well improved containing upwards of 100 acres. The town property will be sold in lots to suit purchasers and liberal credits will be given on the whole, which will be fixed on the day of sale. Also at the same time and place, 5 likely Negroes, for cash in hand, consisting of a woman and 4 children. Also at the same time and place, horses, cattle, hogs, sheep, household and kitchen furniture, framing utensils, corn, hay, oats & c & c., all of which will be sold on liberal credits, and made known on the day of sale, which will take place on the 1st

The Maysville Eagle
day of September next, on the premises and continue from day to day until the whole is disposed of. Due attendance by Stephen M. Vanderen. July 7, '41

State of Kentucky, Bracken Co Sct. George W. Jones, Complainant, against Thomas Moorhead and others, defendants, (Jas. G. Foley and Nath. Foster) in Chancery and Thomas Moorhead Complainant against Geo. W. Jones and other defendants (Jas G. Foley) upon cross bill. The undersigned having been by a decretal of the said court, made at the June term, 1841 appointed a commissioner for the purpose of selling so much of the personal and real property belonging to the late firm of Thomas Moorhead & Co, as shall be of value sufficient to pay and satisfy the said Thomas Moorhead the sum of $2699.93 with interest thereon, at 6 per centum per annual from the 14th day of March 1832 until paid, and also $239.56 the cost of said Moorhead ... expended upon a credit of three months. Also the residue of the real and personal property, for the purpose of paying said Jones the sum of $78,888.57 and the residue if any, then be for the benefit of said Jones, Moorhead & Foley, upon a credit of one, two and three years, equal installments. There will be sold on or near the premises known by the name of Rock Spring on the Ohio River, 4 miles below the town of Augusta and county of Bracken that splendid establishment known by the above name, being an extensive steam flouring mill and distillery, consisting of 341 ½ acres of land, on which is erected a Mill House, 4 stories high, the basement story of stone, the balance from 66 by 40 feet in which are running 6 pair of French Burrs 4 ½ feet diameter, with machinery complete, a large distillery, 60 feet square, 4 stories high, the basement story stone, the balance from,, in compete operation to mash and run 406 bushes of grain per day – the steam engine of sufficient size and power to keep in operation the Mill and Distillery at the same time; two hog pens attached to the distillery sufficient to contain 1500 hogs; a corn crib and warehouse, 100 feet long each and thirty four feet wide, two stories high, comfortably finished, stone or brick chimneys; coopers and clack smith shops and dwelling and tools together with horses, oxen, carts and hogs, about 400 principally small. The mill and distillery are situated at the back of the bottom, about 200 years from the river, to which there is a free McAdamized road. This property standing immediately on the Ohio River, four miles below the beautiful village of Augusta, forty miles above Cincinnati, is so well known from the conspicuous commanding location, that it is deemed unnecessary to indulge in eulogium; every traveler who has passed either up or down the river must have remarked its beautiful and well situated site. Bracken county is one of the best wheat counties in the state, for the number of inhabitants and stock hogs are abundant; cooper's

The Maysville Eagle

stuff is also easily obtained, and barrels are delivered at the most reduced prices. The situation is also considered particularly salubrious immediately opposite the state of Ohio and the fertile counties of Brown and Clemont, rich in the abundance of wheat, corn and hogs. The sale to be on Tuesday the 24th of August next, and continue from day to day until completed from the purchasers, bond and security will be required to have the force and effect of replevin bonds, bearing interest from the date, except sums of $20 and under which is to be for cash in hand. Various other article too numerous to be mentioned in an advertisement. John Burkitt, Com. July 21, 41

To the hemp growers of Mason, Lewis & Fleming Counties. Having purchased the improved and valuable right of Laremer's hemp cradles for cutting hemp, we have now on hand a good assortment of cradles, and will be able to furnish the farmers will all the cradles sufficient to cut their hemp in said counties. This cradle for cutting hemp, can cut double as much as a hook, with equal or less labor, and cut hemp of any length. All orders will be promptly files. H. T. & E. A. Toole, Washington, Mason Co Ky July 3

Wool wanted. The Lewisburg Factory is in full operation, with a large supply of first rate janes on hands, which will be bartered on very favorable terms for wool, or sold low for cash or on short time to punctual men. A few thousand pounds of lambs wool wanted. Lewisburg, July 7, '41

The subscriber adopts this method of calling upon all persons indebted to him, to come forward without delay and make settlement. Those whose notes and accounts are due and of long standing are expected to make immediate payment, without further notice or invitation. Further indulgence cannot be given. F. A. Savage. Minerva, July 3 '41

We expect to go East as early in next month as possible, for a fall and winter supply of goods, and hope our customers will furnish us with the means of doing so. Kirk, Anderson & Sharpe, Maysville, July 31, '41

Trustee's sale. By virtue of deed of trust, executed to us by Isaac Lewis of Mason County, Ky. We will sell at private sale, all the property conveyed in trust to us, consisting of two tracts of land, in Mason county, on the waters of the north Fork of Licking, one continuing 210 acres, adjoining Lewisburg, the other containing 80 acres. Several houses and lots in Lewisburg well improved. One grist mill, 50 by 70 feet, 3 stories high, with 3 run stones, together with a first rate steam engine & one saw mill,

The Maysville Eagle

both in Lewisburg, which run at least 9 months in the year by water. One woolen factory, three stories high, with all the necessary machinery capable of manufacturing 150 yards a day. Several unimproved lots in East Maysville; one pair of carriage horses and barouche; a number of thorough bred durham cattle; several excellent milk cows with calves; 6 head of horses and mares; a lot of hogs; a good stock of farming utensils; blacksmith's tools; 4 or 5000 yards of janes of different qualities; and a quantity of household and kitchen furniture. Those who desire to purchase, will apply to Thomas M. Foreman, near Mayslick, Ky., to Thomas Forman, near Washington, Ky. or to Thomas Y. Brent, of Paris Ky. The property can be seen by application to either of the trustees or to John Tinney, agent at Lewisburg. Thomas M. Forman, Thomas Forman, Thomas Y. Brent. April 28, 1841

A farm for sale. I will sell at public sale, to the highest bidder on Wednesday the 1st day of September next, my farm lying on the road leading to Mayslick, in Murphysville and containing one hundred & eighty seven acres. About one hundred and fifty of which are cleared and in a good state of cultivation. There is on the farm a good dwelling, a fine orchard and an abundance of good water. The terms will be one third in twelve months, and the balance in three years; Possession to be given when the first payment is made. I will also sell, on the same day my farming utensils, one wagon, about one thousand bushels of corn, in the crib, some hay in the stack and my stock, consisting of horses, cattle, (among them a first rate yoke of oxen), hogs and sheep. W. H. Drake July 7, '41

The steam boat, Fairplay. Has changed owners but will still run as a regular packet between Maysville and Cincinnati. It is the intention of the owners to make her a safe, speedy and pleasant boat for passengers. Freights shall be carefully handled and the charge moderate. She will leave Maysville every Monday, Wednesday and Friday at 9o'clock, and Cincinnati on Tuesday, Thursday and Saturday at the same hour. S. Rankin, Master. Sept 12, 1840

Trustee's sale. The undersigned trustees of Milton Dougherty, will sell at private sale a tract of about 380 acres of land, situated on the waters of Lee's Creek, (which contributes to the North Fork of Licking) in Mason County, Kentucky, in which is erected a steam mill, calculated to run by both steam and water and also a distillery. The land lies about five miles from Washington, four miles from Mayslick, and about one half mile from the Maysville and Lexington Turnpike Road. About 250 acres of the tract is cleared and in a good state of cultivation, the balance will timbered and

The Maysville Eagle

set in blue grass. The land will be sold to suit different purchasers if it should be desired. We will also sell at private sale, a number of likely Negroes – also about 160 head of stock hogs; 15 or 50 head of stock cattle and a number of horses and mules. The Negroes and stock are upon the above mentioned farm, where persons who wish to purchase either the land, Negroes or stock, are requested to call and see for themselves. Terms will be made known upon application. Cornelius Drake, Hugh McIlvain. June 9, 1841.

Medical notice. Dr. James Thompson having returned to Mayslick, and permanently located himself there, respectfully tenders his medical services in the various departments of his profession, to the citizens of Mayslick and its vicinity. June 16, '41

The Brandreth Pills. The remarkable cures which have been effected by Brandreth's pills, have astonished the whole medical faculty, many of whom have conceded that they are the greatest blessing that ever was given in the world. Sold by Nolin & Bascom, No. 10 Front Street, Maysville, Ky.

Notice. The partnership heretofore existing between the subscribers in Maysville under the title of Cutter & Jackson, was dissolved by mutual consent on 25 November last. All persons indebted to the late firm, whose notes or accounts are due, are requested to make payment as soon as possible to Henry Cutter & Co, at the old stand occupied by Cutter & Jackson, and who are authorized to settle the business of the late firm. Henry Cutter, David Jackson, Jr. Dec. 10

China & Queensware. George Collins & Co., are receiving (imported by them direct from Liverpool) a large shipment, comprising a general assortment of china and queensware. They will repack to order – unrestricted. A good stock of glassware. Also on hand and for sale, tea, coffee, sugar, molasses, rice, mackerel and salmon, iron nails &c. A lot of wool hats. All sold on fair terms for cash, or at four months time. Undoubted references being furnished. Maysville April 20, 1840

Cigar manufactory. William Hunt, No. 18 Main Cross Street, Maysville, Ky. Has renewed in the rooms next door above Messrs. Leach & Dobyns' warehouse, the manufactory of cigars and will keep constantly on hand a supply of cigars and chewing tobacco, of all kinds which he will sell at wholesale and retail at Cincinnati and Pittsburgh prices. All orders addressed to him directly, or through any of the commission houses of Maysville, will immediately be filled. He respectfully solicits customers of

The Maysville Eagle

merchants and traders, as well as the community generally, assuring them that these articles shall be as good, and his prices fair as any in the market. June 5, 1841

Commissioner's sale. Notice is hereby given by virtue of an interlocutory decree of the Lewis Circuit court, rendered at the June term thereof, 1841, in suit in Chancery therein pending, wherein Charles A. Marshall in complainant and Lewis D. Tolle and James E. Hutchinson, are defendants. The undersigned was appointed a commissioner to make sale of a tract of land, in the county of Lewis, containing 858 1/4 acres, or so much as will be necessary to pay the complainant the sum of $1,889 70cts, together with interest and cost of suit & c. I will on Friday the 27th day of August next offer for sale to the highest bidder, on a credit of six months on the premises at the house of Lewis D. Tolle, the said tract of land, or so much thereof as will be sufficient to pay the complainants debt, interest and cost, mentioned in said decree; the purchaser giving credit with approved security payable to the complainant bearing interest from the day of sale until paid, which bond is to have the force and offer of a sale bond and of execution and the title to be made to the purchaser on the payment of the purchase money. Sale to commence at 11 o'clock a.m. Where due attendance will be given to me. Wm. W. Thomson, commissioner, Lewis County, Ky. Aug. 4, '41.

Extensive Arrivals of spring & summer goods at Kelly's Cash Store. No. 20 Front street Maysville,Ky. The undersigned has just received a large and well assorted stock of British, French and American dry goods, which have been purchased on the very best terms, in the city of New York for cash, and will be sold at prices to suit the times. The stock consists of part of a variety of splendid silks, new patterns....P. H. Kelly

Painting! Painting! Smith & Harman, beg leave respectfully to inform their friends and the public, that they have entered into co-partnership in painting business in Maysville, where they intend to do all kinds of painting, such as house, sign, ornamental and fancy painting. Also, imitations of wood, marble & c. From their long experience in the above business they flatter themselves that they will give entire satisfaction to all who may favor them with their work. A share of public patronage is solicited. Oct 17.

General Agency Commission & Forward Business. A. M. & Wm H. January, of the firm of January, Huston & Co., do hereby tender their thanks to their numerous friends for the very liberal patronage expended to

The Maysville Eagle

the late concern of January, Huston & Co and would respectfully inform them and the public generally that they have this day formed a partnership in this place at the old stand, for the transportation of General Agency Commissions and Forwarding Business, under the firm of A. M. January & Son. Our warehouses are fire-proof, large, convenient and safe in every respect for storing and for sale or to be forwarded. From long experience in the business and our determination to give our close personal attention to the business of the house, we hope to be able to give entire satisfaction to persons considering business to our care. Orders for the purchase of goods or any other articles in this section of country shall at all times have our prompt attention. A. M. January, Wm. H. January, Maysville, Ky. July 23, 1840

To Rent. A farm of two hundred and eighty-eight acres of land, lying on the bank of the Ohio River, in the county of Lewis above the mouth of Kinnekennick, known by the name of Forman's Bottom. Any person wishing to rent the said farm can learn the terms by applying to A. A. Wadsworth or myself in the city of Maysville. James N. Morrison. Feb 27, 1841

Music. G. W. Blaetterman, professor of music, offers his services to the citizens of Maysville. He will give lessons on the piano, violin and guitar. Terms $12 per quarter. He will also give instruction in modern languages to wit; French, Italian, Spanish and German. March 10, 1841

Removal. John C. Reed, has removed his copper, tin and sheet iron ware manufactory, to the warehouse formerly occupied by William Ficklen, on Market street, four doors below his old stand, where he will continue to keep a large assortment of wares of the best quality, which he will positively sell at the Pittsburgh prices, and on as good as terms as they can be had any where. His long and well tried experience in business, together with a number of experienced workmen in his employ, will enable him to execute all orders with neatness and dispatch, and he pledges himself that his work shall not be excelled in quality of material, workmanship or cheapness. Purchasers are invited to call and examine for themselves. Improved premium cooking stoves, coal and wood stoves. Fancy, common and coal grates of all sizes, kept constantly for sale by John C. Reed. March 11, 1840

Losses promptly paid. Maysville Insurance Company. Continue to take risks on goods, wares and merchandize, and produce of every description against fire – also, on cargoes on steam, keel or flat boats, on any of the

The Maysville Eagle

rivers, lakes, bayous, or canals, or from any one port in the United States to that of another. They also make insurances on lives, grant annuities and make contracts in which the casualties of life are involved. A. M. January President, Ric'd Henry Lee, Wm. M. Poyntz, Christian Shultz, Richard Collins, Thomas Y Payne, Thos. R. Robertson, directors, Matthew Markland, Secretary. January 3, 1841

Produce Agency, commission & forwarding business George M. Procter, has opened a forwarding and commission warehouse net door to Messrs. Pearce, Fant & Brodrick's wholesale dry goods store and 3rd door above the Maysville Insurance Office on Main Cross Street, where he will give his personal attention to any consignment that he may be entrusted to his care. He will pay particular attention to the sales of country produce, he will in addition to his commission house, have a hemp house where he will bale hemp and make sales to the best advantage for the interest of the farmers. Maysville, Nov 18, 1840. References. John D. Davis & Co. Pittsburg, Pa, Dorsey & Armstrong, Wheeling, Va., Phillips, Reynolds & Co., Louisville, Ky. Hughart & Dickerson, Paris, Ky. H. N. Davis & Co., St. Louis, Mo.

Land on the Ohio River for sale. I wish to sell the farm on which I now live, four miles above Maysville, on the Ohio River, on the Kentucky side. This tract contains about 80 acres on which are comfortable improvements, good fruit, water & c. It is the place on which Benj. Reynolds, dec'd formerly lived, and more recently owned and occupied by Wm. R. Mitchell. Also, on other tract, one and a half miles above this tract, also living immediately on the Ohio River, occupied at present by Wm. ? Mitchell. This tract contains about 63 acres on which is a comfortable dwelling, and out houses, good water & c. Each of these will be sold on good terms. For further particulars inquire of M. Markland in Maysville, who is authorized to make sale. John M. Clarke. March 28, 1840

Cigars, Tobacco & Snuff, selling at reduced prices. The undersigned intending to close his cigar store this fall, will dispose of his stock now on hand, consisting of a large lot of superior Spanish, half Spanish and Kentucky cigars. Chewing tobacco and snuff, all of which he will sell at wholesale or retail, at lower prices than the same quality of articles can be had in the city. The way to test it is to call and see. All orders thankfully received and promptly attended to. James G. Spalding, No. 8, Front Street, Maysville. June 9, 1841.

Notary Public Notice. Charles B. Ryan, of Maysville, Ky. Having been duly commissioned and sworn as a Notary Public, for the county of Mason,

The Maysville Eagle is prepared to issue letters of protest and to attend to any business appertaining to that office, May 8, 1841.

New Goods. Anderson & Sharpe, No. 11, Front Street, have just received from the Eastern cities a large and general assortment of British, French, India, German and American staple and fancy dry goods, adapted to the present and approaching seasons, of the most fashionable and substantial kinds, which make their stock now complete. This stock of goods was purchased at low prices, and carefully selected by one of the concern, and will be sold of corresponding low prices, and at the lowest possible rates, for cash, or good paper to punctual dealers. They respectfully solicit the patronage of their friends and an examination of their goods by all wishing to purchase. Maysville, April 7, 1841

The undersigned, a committee appointed by the city council, would respectfully solicit proposals from the mechanics, for the building of two school houses, for the accommodation of the City Free Schools; one to be located upon the lower end of the city property near the Alms House – the other to be located in the lower end of the city, upon some spot to be designated. The house is to be of the following dimensions. Forty feet in length and thirty feet wide, one story high, built of brick, the walls 9 inches thick, with a chimney or flue at each end, two doors and eight windows. The undersigned also solicit a donation of ground from the property holders, on which to place the lower school house. The proposals will be in writing and directed to the undersigned. Tho. Y. Payne, S. B. Nicholson, Francis T. Hord, Maysville, May 12.

For Sale. The whole stock or half of drugs, medicines, paints, oils, glass, instruments & c & c. on hand, comprising almost every article, with few exceptions of a couple assortments, is offered for sale on good terms, for cash and credit made secure. The house has been in operation for six years, is a good stand; anyone understanding the business and wishing to settle himself a business, would do well to call and see for themselves, as I will sell on fair terms. Wishing to settle up all transactions of the house, I have come to the conclusion at this will be the best method. Also, all those indebted, I hope will not let me have to dun them so often, but fork over, and that will enable me to do the same. J. W. Johnston, Druggist, No 10, Market Street, Maysville, March 6, 1841.

Just received a superior lot of Spanish cigars, assorted brands, also a fresh supply of paints, drystuff, drugs & c. Dr. A. Seaton. March 17, 1841

The Maysville Eagle

Removal. Jacob Outten, Jr. Has removed his stove, tin & sheet iron ware manufactory, to the house adjoining Rounds & Reed's from the river, where he will keep articles principally of his own make, warranted to be good. Persons wishing any article or articles in his line of business, would do well to call and examine for themselves. Superior blacking kept constantly on hand for sale. Maysville, May 30, '40

Valuable Farm for sale, on the waters of Mill Creek, in Mason Co. A farm of about 175 acres, having up on it an indifferent dwelling, a good barn and other necessary buildings, will be sold upon good terms, if application made in time. 75 acres of it is finely timbers. The whole unsurpassed in quality. John S. Forman. Nov 6, 1839

Tobacco and hemp warehouse. The subscriber having taken the establishment of Wm. B. Mocklar & Co. on 3rd street, intends to continue the manufacture of tobacco as usual, where he will at all time keep, a supply of tobacco of various kinds. He is also prepared to receive and bale hemp, leaf tobacco & c. D. Spalding, Jr. Maysville, March 23, 1839

New wholesale stove warehouse and manufactory of tin, copper, brass and sheet-iron wares of every description by Richard Reed, on Market Street, next door to Simon Nelson's. All kind of job work in tin copper & sheet-iron, done in the best manner and at fair prices such as house-roofing, spouting, valeytin and making and repairing copper pipes for steam mills, distilleries & c. Also cooking stoves by the single or dozen, with or without trimming to suit country tinners or merchants, at Cincinnati prices. Feb. 10, 1841

Sperm candles. 10 boxes sperm candles, best quality, 10 bags pepper, for sale by A. M. January & Son. Maysville, 31st March, '41

The subscribers have succeeded to the business of the late house of Cutter & Jackson, and are prepared to do a general wholesale liquor, wine and grocery business under the title of Henry Cutter & Co at the old stand lately occupied by Cutter & Jackson corner of Second and Sutton Streets, Maysville, Ky., where may always be found large and well selected assortment of Goods in their line which they will sell low for cash, barter or on 4 months credit to those who will pay punctually. Henry Cutter, Hamilton Gray, Dec 19

Commission Warehouse. The undersigned having commenced the above business on Wall Streets, convenient to the Steam-boat landing on the lower

The Maysville Eagle

grade, solicits the patronage of this friends and the public generally. He is also prepared to bale hemp and press tobacco. Empty tobacco hogs heads kept constantly on hand. O. H. Davis. Maysville, March 24.

Fresh supply of boards & shingles, which I will sell low for cash, or on short credit. James K. Ficklin, Maysville, April 28, 1841

Maysville, Ky., Wednesday March 27, 1844 The Maysville Eagle, by Collins & Brown. At two dollars and fifty cents in advance. Three dollars in six months, or three dollars and fifty cents at the end of the year.

J. S. Hall, Esq. late one of the editors of the Kentucky tribune, has taken charge of the editorial department of the "Southron," published at Jackson, Miss.

Death of Fairfield, the poet – Sumner Lincoln Fairfield, well known as the author of several beautiful poems, died in New Orleans on the 7th inst. Hi harp has been unstrung on earth, but to be attuned, we trust, to nobler and sweeter sons in heaven. \

Russell, the vocalist, is giving concerts in Nashville.

The Buckeye – Captain Caldwell, of the Buckeye, has instituted a suit in the United States District court, for Louisiana, against the owners of the De Soto, for damages to the amount of $10,000. General Felix Huston is counsel for the plaintiff.

Stabbing. – The Osage (Mo.) Yeoman, of the 7^m inst., says that the Hon. B.P. Mayer, Senator from that district, has been stabbed with a small knife a few days before by Elijah Cherry. Mr. Mayer's situation was deemed very critical. Cherry had been examined and discharged.

George R. McKee, Esq. has been appointed by Governor Letcher, Judge of the 19th Judicial District of this State, in place of Hon. John White, declined. A better appointment and one which will afford more general satisfaction could not have been made. Mr. McKee is an able lawyer, and a courteous and honorable gentleman. We have known his long and well, and we take pleasure in saying that, in our humble opinion, he has few superiors in Kentucky in point of talents, and we know of none in whose bosom glows more fervently the principles of honor and justice.

The Maysville Eagle

We are indebted to the politeness of Mr. J. P. Jack, Clerk of the S. B. Hibernia, for late Pittsburg papers.

Hon. John White – The Cincinnati Gazette pays the following deserved compliment to the Hon. John White of this state: This excellent man, and consistently virtuous politician has been appointed by the Governor of Kentucky. Judge of the 19th Judicial Circuit of that State. He declines We are glad of it. The South needs more such men in as Mr. Ex-Speaker White in Congress – men who can look beyond the passion of the hour to her real good, and the good of the country. He is a sound, considerate, American – firm, liberal and just in action, as well as in opinion.

Snow – we had another heavy fall of snow at this city yesterday morning.

J. P. Johnson, late postmaster at Danville, Ky has absconded to parts unknown, leaving his wife destitute, and taking with him some three or four hundred dollars of "Uncle Sam's" money.

The Blacksmith, at the Battle of Bradywine. And now I have given you some instances of courage and heroic daring among those high in station and renowned in fame. One instance more – an example of reckless courage. The hero was a stout blacksmith – aye, a humble blacksmith, but his stout frame, hardened by toil, throbbed with as generous an impulse of freedom as ever beat in the bosom of a Lafayette, or throbbed around the heart of a mad Anthony Wayne. It was in the full tide of retreat, that a follower of the American camp, who had at least shouldered a car-whip in his country's services, was driving a baggage wagon from the battle field, while some short distance behind a body of Continentals were rushing forward, with a troop of Britishers in close pursuit. The wagon had arrived at a narrow point of the bye road leading to the south, where two high banks of rock and crag arising on either side, affording just space sufficient for the passage of the wagon, and not an inch more. His eye was arrested by the sight of a stout muscular man, some forty years of age, extended at the foot of a tree at the very opening of this pass. He was clad in the course attire of a mechanic. His coat had been flung aside, and with the shirt sleeves rolled up from his muscular arms, he lay extended on the turf, with his rifle in his grasp while the blood streamed in a torrent from his right leg broken at the knee by a cannon ball. The wagoner's sympathies were arrested by the sight – he would have paused in the very instant of his flight, and placed the wounded blacksmith in his wagon, but the stout hearted mechanic refused. "I'll not get into his wagon," he exclaimed in his rough way; "but I'll tell you what I will do. You see yonder cherry tree on the top of that rock that hangs over the road? Do you think you could lift a man of my build up thar? For you see, neighbor, " he continued, while the blood flowed from his wound, " I never meddled with the Britishers until they came trampling over this valley and burned my house down. But now I'm all riddled to pieces and haint got more than fifteen minutes life in me! But I have got three good rifle balls in my cartridge box, and so jist prop me up against that cherry tree, and I'll give 'em the whole three shots and then," he exclaimed, " and then I'll die!" The wagoner started his horses ahead, and then with a sudden effort of strength, dragged the blacksmith along the sod to the foot of the cherry tree surmounting the rock by the road side. In a moment the back was propped against the tree, his face was to the advancing troopers, and while his shattered leg hand over the bank, the wagoner rushed on his way, while the blacksmith very coolly proceeded to load his rifle. It was not long before a body of American soldiers rushed by with the British in pursuit. The blacksmith greeted them with a shout, and then raising his rifle to his shoulder, he picked the foremost from hi steed, with the exclamation, "that's for Gen. Washington" In a moment the rifle was loaded again was it fired, and the pursuing British rode over the body of another fallen officer: "That's for myself!" cried the blacksmith. And then with a hand strong with the feeling of coming death, the sturdy freeman again loaded, again raised his rifle. He fired his last shot, and as another officer kissed the sod, the tear quivered in the eye of the dying blacksmith, "And that" he cried with a husky voice which strengthened into a shout, "And that's for Mad Anthony Wayne!" Long after the battle was past, the body was discovered, propped against the tree, with the feature, frozen in death, smiling grimly, whilst the right hand grasped the never failing rifle. And thus died one of the ten thousand brave mechanic heroes of the revolution. Brave in the hour of battle; undaunted in the hour of retreat; undismayed in the hour of death. Citizen Soldier

Marriages. On Wednesday evening last by Elder G. Mason, Henry W. Wood, Esq. to Miss Hannah Jane Lashbrooke, all of Washington.

On the 7th inst. By the same, Mr. David Davis, to Miss Susan Finch, all of the county.

Valuable Mason Farm for sale. The subscribers as Trustees for the creditors of William Bickley, offer for sale the farm whereon the said Bickley resides, in Mason County, Ky. The tract contains upwards of 500 acres, is handsomely improved, having a neat dwelling house, barn, cribs, stables, ice house, a new horse mill for grinding meal, and corn in the ear;

The Maysville Eagle

a young orchard of excellent fruit trees, and all the conveniences necessary for a farm of the size. It is situated two and a half miles south of Maysville and one and a half east of Washington, and between the Maysville & Lexington and Maysville & Mountsterling Turnpike Roads, and abutting on the latter. There are about 360 acres of cleared land and the remainder of the tract is well timbered; 220 acres of the cleared land is in excellent condition for the cultivation of hemp. It is admirably calculated for a stock farm, also producing excellent grass and well watered. Its proximity to the city of Maysville and the facility with which that market can be reached the fertility of the soil, and its high healthy situation, render it one of the most desirable farms in Northern Kentucky. The title is indisputable. Any one wishing to purchase, can examine the premises by calling upon the subscriber, Mr. Bickley, who yet resides upon them. We are anxious to dispose of the farm at private sale, consequently the terms will be a matter of contract between the purchaser and the trustees. Robert T. Blanchard, H. Taylor. January 31, 1844

For Sale. A house and lot for sale, in the town of Lexington, Lafayette County, Missouri, suitable for a large family, or a Public House, and at this time kept as one, and is considered as good a stand as any in the state for that business. For terms apply to Wm. B. Waddell, in Lexington or Charles Scudder, in St. Louis. February 28, 1844

New Establishment. The undersigned begs leave to inform the citizens of Maysville and the public generally, that he has just opened at No. 24, Front Street, a new hat, cap & shoe store, where he will keep constantly on hand a large assortment of hats, caps and shoes of every description, which he will sell as low for cash, as they can be purchased in any city in the West. His friends are earnestly invited to give him a call. James Wormald. Maysville, August 23, 1843

Henrie House. The subscriber, J. B. Young, late of New York and formerly proprietor of the United States Hotel, in the city of Buffalo, has taken this well known and popular establishment, which he is now repairing and newly furnishing in a manner and style not surpassed by any in the western country – and from his long experience in the business he feels confident he shall fully sustain the former reputation of the house. The location being in the center of business in this flourishing Queen City of the West, he hopes to meet a good share of patronage. Prices to suit the times. J. B Young, proprietor. J. W. Young & Wm. P. Young, Superintendents, Cincinnati, March 13, 1844

The Maysville Eagle

F. T. Chambers & H. R. Reeder, attorneys at law. Have removed their office to the old bank building in Washington. Having secured the assistance of an eminent attorney in Frankfort, all cases in Bankruptsey entrusted to them will be promptly carried through. Washington, Oct 15, 1842

Late Arrival. Just received at No 9 Front Street a few pieces splendid Velvet Bonnet Ribbons, plain, green, brown, claret, olive, cirtron, gimps, various colors; plain cloth shawls; heavy cassimeres, & c. & c. Kirk & Fant. Maysville, Nov. 11, 1843

A Mitchell's Improved patent Washing Machine. Patented No. 6, 1843. As this machine has been but recently invented, it may be necessary to say that it combines great durability, ease of motion and simplicity; not liable to get out of order, and is sold at a price to suit the hard times – washes fast, does it well, without rubbing or injuring the clothes. Manufactured at the patentee's shop in Aberdeen, Ohio, where they are for sale and at John B. McIlvain's Warehouse in Maysville.

Wagon Making. John Matchet respectfully informs the citizens of Maysville and its vicinity, that he has opened a shop on Second, immediately below Short Street, where he is prepared to do all kinds of work on wagons & c. From 20 years experience at the business, he flatters himself that he will receive a share of the public patronage. All kinds of turning can be had at the same shop. Maysville, Nov. 25, 1843

Cash Store. New Goods. Rees & Allen have just received and opened on Front Street a large assortment of fine and fashionable goods consisting of all the variety of styles and quality suitable for the fall and winter trade. We do not think it necessary to specify the quantity or kind, as our stock is very large. We solicit persons wishing to purchase to call and examine our goods as we think we can make it their interest to do so. We will sell very low for cash. Rees & Allen. Maysville, Nov. 25, 1843

Watches & Jewelry. A. W. Bascom has just received from Philadelphia and New York, a splendid assortment of gold and silver patent lever watches, of every variety & quality; gold fob and guard chains; spectacles, pencils and thimbles, splendid topaz, ruby and garnet breastpins, bracelets and finger rings, set and plain gold studs, hair pins, silver pencils, spectacles and butter knives, Rodgers' & Wostenholm's pocket & pen knives, Razors and Razor Straps, Guil'ott's Steel Pens, coral necklaces, which together with his fomer stock, constitutes the largest assortment of watches and jewelry ever

The Maysville Eagle
offered for sale in this city, comprising all the variety usually kept in establishments of the kinds and will be sold as low as they can be purchased in Cincinnati or any other place in the West. Watches repaired and warranted to perform. A large assortment of silver spoons constantly kept on hand. No. 17 Front Street, Maysville, Ky January 29, 1844

New Goods. We are now receiving our spring and summer stock of goods, comprising two hundred and fifty packages of foreign and domestic dry goods, among which will be found everything in the dry goods line, of the latest patterns and styles. L. C. & H. T. Pearce. Maysville, March 9, 1844

Watches & Jewelry. The subscriber has just received, direct from New York, a splendid assortment of gold and silver watches, fold chains, seals and keys, fine stone rings, enameled pins, single stone pins, custer broches, bracelet, lockets, bracelet clasps, gold studs, gold and silver pencils, gold and silver spectacles. Thimbles, Silver butter knives, silver guard chains, German silver spoons, fine penknives and scissors. (Wostenbolm & sons) and (rogers) make; steel pens, silk purses, tooth picks, spectacle glasses & c. together with a variety of other articles, which were selected by himself, all new and fashionable goods and will be sold at very low prices. Clocks and watches repaired in the best manner. D. S. Hudson, Corner of River and Market St. Maysville, January 6, 1843.

Accidental Death. A young man named Shelton Gully, of Garrard County, whilst engaged, on Sunday last, in loading a boat with hogsheads of tobacco,, at the mouth of Sugar Creek, got his head between two of them, by which it was crushed and his death instantaneously produced. Rich. Ky. Chron.

Family Bibles for sale at Edward Cox No. 5 Front Street, March 16, 1844

A large assortment of dye stuff, paints, oils, varnishes & c. & c., all of which I offer for sale on the lowest possible terms. Wm. R. Wood, Druggist, Corner of Market & Water Streets, Maysville, August 30, 1843

Cheap Books, Eagle Bookstore

Powder, 40 kegs rifle powder, 15 kegs blasting powder. Just received and for sale by W & N Poyntz

An ordinance concerning boarding houses. Be it ordained that the ordinance approved by the council on the 9th day of October, 1839, shall not be construed to extend to persons keeping boarding houses. But the law as to boarding houses shall remain as by ordinance, approved 19^{m} Aril, 1833. Approved in Council, 7th March 1844 Richard Collins, B. C. C. James A. Lee, City Clerk, March 23, 1844

Females Beware!!! It is an indisputable fact, demanding serious and solemn consideration, that thousands of the fairest and loveliest of the female sex fall yearly into an untimely grave. The unconscious victims of their own suicidal acts! From the registers of mortality, we find the deaths of females too far exceed those of males and that the greatest portion died in the bloom of youth, before they attain the age of twenty five. Yes twenty! Consumption is a disease that spreads its insidious ravages throughout the universe and nips both great and small, listen then to a warning voice which echoes constantly in your ears, and guard yourself from the first unerring seed of this disease which is certain to knit its fatal threads and hurry you to the solitary tomb! As the rattlesnake it warns you of its poisonous fangs and you heed it not, until the sting o death is fast riveted in your system. It is only at this time, for the first your will begin to be concerned about your health; but it may be too late. May these facts awaken you from your slumbers, and cause you to listen to the solemn voice of reason, and use the medicine that has prolonged and preserved the lives of thousands when used in time. Dr. Duncan's Expectorant Remedy, Sold in Maysville at the Eagle Book Store. March 23, 1844

Maysville, Ky., Wednesday October 16, 1844

Odd Fellows. The Independent Order of Odd Fellows had quite an agreeable celebration in this city on Thursday last The turnout of members was large and respectable and the procession presented an imposing appearance. After marching through the principal streets of the city, accompanied by the Cincinnati Brass Band of music, and the Maysville band, the procession repaired to the Methodist Church, where a beautiful and chaste address on the principles of the Order was delivered by Rev. G. G. Moore of Covington, Ky. The procession then proceeded to the dinner, which was prepared in excellent style by W. B. Parker, Esq. It was abundant and of the best quality. H. B. Brown presided on the occasion, and Rev. Mr. Light acted as Chaplain. After the cloth was moved a number of sentiments were read and received with hearty cheers. The whole proceedings were conducted with great propriety and reflected the highest credit on the Order.

The Maysville Eagle

Marriages. On Thursday evening, the 10th inst., by Elder Lewis Jacobs, Mr. John Holiday, to Miss Alvira Harrison, all of this city.

Deaths. Died on the 30th ultimo, at the residence of Hugh J. Brent Esq., in Bourbon County, Mr. John J. Chambers, son of the Hon. John Chambers, Governor of Iowa, aged about 19 years.

Valuable Land and Mill Property for Sale. The Pleasant Valley Mills near the mouth of Fleming Creek, Nicholas County, being a Grist and Saw Mill, propelled by water, both new and in first rate order; together with near 100 acres of land, a goodly portion of which is first rate, with a dwelling house and out houses of the best and most convenient character. The Grist Mill is constructed both for merchant and country work, is an excellent flowering mill and will run more or less all the year by water power alone. It would also be an excellent position for a carding factory and tan yard – there is a first rate store house and a good stand for retailing dry goods, groceries & c., The property being situated near Licking River a lasting resource for Poplar and Pine Timber of the best quality. The proprietor is determined to sell and expects to sell low. Purchasers will please call and examine for themselves. The property possesses many advantages in its locality which can be seen better than described. Terms will be made known by the subscriber. R. S. Carter. Pleasant Valley, August 3rd, 1844

Great Bargain. The subscriber offers for sale a tract of land, situated on the Ohio River, adjoining the town of Chilo, in Clermont Co., Ohio, thirty-six miles above Cincinnati, containing from one hundred and eighty-five to three hundred and twenty acres. The land is in a good state of cultivation, with all necessary buildings & c., and a large portion first rate River Bottom Immediate possession and a first rate bargain will be given if application be made soon, as I am determined to sell. John O. Prather. June 5, 1844

Boots & Shoes by the package – cheap for cash. The subscriber is prepared to sell good quality boots, shoes and brogans of every description, as low as they can be bought of the manufacturer. Purchasers are requested to examine the market, and then call at No. 69 Chestnut, below Third Street, Philadelphia. Thomas L Evans.

J. A. M'Clung & H. Taylor, Attorneys at Law, Washington, Kentucky. Will hereafter practice law in partnership in the Mason Circuit. Jan 1, 1843

The Maysville Eagle

New Goods, At Wholesale and Retail. The undersigned have just received and opened on Front Street a large store of Fall and Winter Goods. Armstrong & Collins. Maysville, Sept 14, 1844

Removal, Dr. Shackleford has removed his office to 3rd street one door above his residence, and three doors below Market Street, where he may be consulted when not absent on professional business. Maysville, Feb.7, 1844

E. C. Phister, Attorney at Law, Maysville, Ky. Will practice in the Courts of Mason and the adjoining counties, and in the court of appeals. Office on Sutten Street in the second story of R. H. Lee's Cotton Store. May 8, 1844

Professional Notice. Dr. Throop having returned to Mayslick, offers his professional services to his old friends and the citizens generally and will be found there at all times except when professionally engaged. Mayslick, April 17, '44

Thomas H. Nelson, (late of Kentucky.) Rockville, Indiana has been appointed by the Governor, Commissioner for the State of Kentucky, to take within the State of Indiana, Acknowledgements of Deeds, Mortgages, Contracts, Letters of Attorney and other writings under Seal, to be used or recorded in the State of Kentucky. Also to administer Oaths or Affirmations and to make any affidavit to be used in said State. Also to take depositions in any suit depending in any court in said state. R. W. Thompson, of Virgo. T H. Nelson, of Parke. Thompson & Nelson, attorneys at Law, Rockville, Indiana, Will attend to the collection of Debts throughout the Wabash Valley, July 17th, 1844

John N. Furber, Attorney and Counselor at Law, Brooksville, Bracken County, Ky. Will promptly attend to all business entrusted to him, throughout the Judicial district. December 8, '41

Fall and Winter Goods, we are now receiving our stock for the fall and winter trade, embracing almost every article that is new and desirable for both ladies and gentlemen's wear.... Kirk & Fant.

Fall and Winter Goods, at No. 11 Front Street, Maysville, Ky. I am just receiving from the Eastern market, a new and complete assortment of fall and winter goods, of the best qualities and latest styles, all of which are for sale on favorable terms, and request an examination of the same, by those

The Maysville Eagle

wishing to purchase. Further promises I consider unnecessary. Ely D. Anderson, Maysville, Oct. 2, 1844

Window Sash for sale. Morris A. Hutchins has just received in addition to his former stock of Window Sash The whole will be sold extremely low for cash. June 5th 1844

Hats & Caps. Just received at the Hat & "Cap Store, No. 24, Front Street, a large and well assorted stock of hats & caps, of the latest and most approved style. The public are respectfully invited to call and examine the stock, which is believed to be more complete and offers better inducements than any in the city. James Wormald. Maysville, Sept. 18, 1844

William P. Conwell, Attorney and Counselor at Law, Maysville, Kentucky. Will practice in the Circuit Courts of Mason and the adjoining Counties; the U. S. District and Circuit Courts for the State of Kentucky and the Court of Appeals. Office, No. 23, Front Street, June 4, 1842

N. S. Dimmitt, Attorney at Law, Lewisburg, Ky. Will practice in the Magistrates County and Circuit Courts for Mason, May 3rd, '43

Henry Waller, Attorney and Counselor at Law. Maysville, Ky. Will practice in the Courts of Mason and the adjoining Counties and in the Court of Appeals. Office immediately over the Maysville Insurance Office, on Main Cross Street. July 27, 1844

Cabinet Ware Room, No. 18, East Fourth between Main & Sycamore streets, Cincinnati. Jones & Rammelsberg, Cincinnati, Sept. 25, 1844

Nicholas Farm for Sale. I offer to sell my farm in Nicholas County, on the road from Hawkin's Mill on Licking to Moorfield, 9 miles east of Carlisle, 2 ½ from Licking, and 3 from Moorfield, containing 272 or 3 acres of first rate land, 200 acres cleared and under fence, a portion in grass. The improvements are good, a good 1 ½ story brick dwelling house and other suitable buildings, there is a good spring, and plenty of stock water. I will make the terms such as to offer great inducements to such as wish to purchase a home. I am determined to sell, and would advise those who may wish to purchase to make application immediately to me near Sharpsburg, to Gen. Wm. Sudduth, near the same place, or to L. M Cox, at Flemingsburg. Thomas J. Fields. Sharpsburg, Sept. 7, 1844

The Maysville Eagle

Essays on Practical Agriculture, By A. Beatty. This valuable work is now for sale, by the dozen or single, at the Eagle Book Store. Every farmer of Kentucky should immediately supply himself with a copy. September 1844

Fall and Winter Goods. I have just received my stock of fall and winter goods, which is large and complete and I can and will sell as low as any house in the city. I would warn my friends and the public not to be gulled by the lengthy advertisements which occasionally appear, it is generally the case that the man who is most extravagant in promises performs the least. Jos. F. Brodrick. Maysville, Ky. Sept 14, 1844

Valuable Mason Farm for Sale. I wish to sell the farm on which I now reside, containing 350 acres of first rate land, situate one mile North of Washington, the County Seat, three miles from the City of Maysville, and within two hundred yards of the Maysville and Lexington Turnpike Road. Upwards of 100 acres wood land, all enclosed and never failing springs. Any person wishing a desirable farm would do well to come and look at it. Tho's Forman. May 18, 1844

W. T. Reid, Attorney at Law, Maysville, Kentucky. Office on Market Street, opposite the warehouses of Wm. & N. Poyntz; Will faithfully attend to any business which may be entrusted to him in Mason, or any of the adjoining Counties. January 14, 1843

Slaughtering Hogs. We have enlarged our extensive pork house, and are now prepared to kill and pack five hundred hogs per day. We will furnish barrels, kegs and salt at the lowest moderate price. Our establishment will be ready by the first day of November. Any one wishing to pack pork will find it to their interest to give us a call. W. & N. Poyntz. Maysville, October 7, 1844

Tapers. Cheap light for the sick chamber, just received at No. 10 Market Street. M. A. Adamson, Sept. 28, 1844

Stop the thief and runaway! $200 reward. Ranaway from the subscriber, living in Fayette County, near Centreville, on the morning of the 12th inst. A Negro Man named Peter, 24 years old, 5 feet 8 or 9 inches high, very black and weighs about 160 pounds. He has squint eyes. He had with him when he left, a pair of saddle-bags. He will probably try to get into the state of Ohio. I will pay the above reward if said boy is taken out of the state of Kentucky. $100 if taken in any of the counties bordering on the Ohio River, or $20 if taken in any county adjoining Fayette, and secured in

The Maysville Eagle

jai so that I get him, and word conveyed to me at Centreville, Bourbon Co. Ky. Jacob Sidener, Sr. Sept. 28, 1844

Cheap umbrellas & Parasols, Wholesale and Retail. At N. L. Cole, East Fifth street, near Main Street Cincinnati.

Brush Manufactory and Wire Store, No. 106 Main Street between Third and Fourth, Cincinnati, Butcher and M'Laughlin.

Negro Woman Wanted. I will pay cash for a Negro Woman, from 18 to 25 years old, who is a good cook, washes, ironer and house servant. Apply to the subscriber on Tuckahoe Ridge. John Masterson. Mason Co., Sept. 25, 1844

Commissioner's Sale, of land in Mason County, Under a decree of the Mason Circuit Court, rendered at the recent August term, in the suit of Peter Harrison's adm'r vs. Peter Harrison's heirs and creditors, I shall as commissioner of said court on the 22 day of Oct next at the Tavern House of the late Peter Harrison, dec'd on the Maysville and Mountsterling Turnpike Road, near the town of Lewisburgh, Mason County, Kentucky, offer for sale at public auction to the highest bidder, on a credit of one year for the last payment of the purchase money, three tracts of land, the first containing about 100 acres on which the tavern stand is situated and where Peter Harrison and Dominick Harrison formerly resided. The second tract in the Oak Woods and within about two miles of the first named tract. The 50 acres will be sold subject to the dower of the widow of Peter Harrison, dec'd and which has been laid off to her. The purchaser or purchasers will be required to give bond with good personal security for the payment of the purchase money, bearing interest from the day of sale, and a lien will be retained upon the lands to secure the ultimate payment of the purchase money. Sale will commence between the hours of 11 o'clock, a.m. and 2 o'clock, p.m. Chas. Clarke, Com'r. Sept. 21, 1844

Commissioner's Sale, of land on Lees Creek, lots in East Maysville, Negroes & Personal Property. Under a decree of the Mason Circuit Court, rendered at the last August term, in the suit of Joseph Watson vs. G. Y. Reynolds and others, I shall on the 25th day of October next, at the residence of Joseph Watson, on Lees Creek, Mason County, Ky. offer for sale at public auction to the highest bidder, on a credit of one year for the first and two years for the second payment of the purchase money, the tract of land whereon the said Watson reside. I shall, at the time and place offer for sale, to the highest bidder on a credit of six months, six valuable slaves

The Maysville Eagle

and a quantity of personal property, the later consisting of horses, cattle, sheep, hogs, farming utensils and household and kitchen furniture. And on the 26th day of October next, I shall offer for sale at public auction to the highest bidder, on the premises in Maysville, on a credit of one year for one held and two years for the other half of the purchase money, two lots in East Maysville, belonging to the estate of Zephaniah Watson, dec'd. Purchasers will be required to give bonds with good personal security for the purchase money, bearing interest from the date. Ja's McMillin, Com'r. September 14, 1844

Valuable Real and Personal Estate for Sale. The undersigned as Executor of Daniel Ficklin, deceased, will expose to sale at Public Auction, on Thursday, the 24th of October, at the late residence of the deceased in Fleming County, on the road from the Upper Blue Lick to Little Sandy Salt Works, two miles from the Poplar Plains. The farm on which said Ficklin resided in his life time, containing 225 or 230 acres. About 175 acres cleared, under good fence, and in a high state of cultivation; a good dwelling house and out buildings, a first rate barn, and stables sufficient for fifty head of horses, an excellent apple orchard – the farm is well watered – title indisputable. Also, Cattle, horses, sheep, hogs, farming utensils, a good four horse wagon and gear, an excellent yoke of oxen, household and kitchen furniture, corn in the crib and field, wheat, oat and hay & c. & c., Sale to commence at 9 o'clock a.m. and continue from day to day, until all the property is sold. Terms of land will be made known on the day of sale. The personal property will be sold on a credit of twelve months, the purchaser giving bond and approved security. Sums under five dollars, cash in hand. Daniel Ficklin, Executor. October 2, 1844

Fire Setts, polished steel shovel, tongs & pokers. For sale at the house of N. D. Hunter, no 20 Front St, Oct. 5, 1844

Dover, Ky. Oct 14, 1844. Messrs. Collins & Brown: You may assure our friends of Ohio, Indiana, Pennsylvania and Kentucky, that the Whigs of Dover and vicinity are fully aroused and are determined to spare no effort to have a spirited meeting on the 23rd inst. The spirit of '40 is awake. The Committee of Arrangements have appointed Col. Stephen Lee & A. Soward chief Marshals and Col. Samuel Worthington, Capt. W. D. Coryvell, Maj. Wm. Bickley and Dr. Basil Duke, Assistant Marshals. J. J. Anderson, Ch'n Com. Arrangements.

Suicides and Murders in Vicksburg. Mrs. Beagley, of Vicksburg, a respectable Irish widow lady and a school teacher having several children,

The Maysville Eagle
committed suicide on the 14th ult. By cutting her throat with a razor. The coroner's jury reported that she probably killed herself to escape the promulgation of her shame. We regard such a verdict as an unpardonable outrage.

On the 17th ult. Mrs. Vogel of Vicksburg the wife of a German painter, terminated her own life and that of her two children, one about three years and the other one year old, by hanging. The disheartened husband had been absent but one hour and a half. She is said to have been driven to the terrible deed by jealousy. Mr. V. is spoken of as an honest, industrious, and peaceable man.

For the Maysville Eagle. Messrs. Collins & Brown, in justice to the "Franklin Insurance Company of Louisville,' and for the benefit of the public, we give the following statement. We had insured by J. P. Dobyns, agent of the above company in Maysville, 5000 dollars on our stock of goods, from Pittsburgh to Maysville, a part of which were on the steam boat Adelaide, when she sunk. On the arrival of our damaged goods at Maysville, we were immediately advised by our agent, and one of our firm forthwith visited Maysville to give the matter attention. In less then two hours after his arrival, our loss was satisfactorily adjusted, and promptly paid by the agent. There was no disposition manifested to quibble or delay the matter, but on the contrary every disposition to settle fairly and promptly, which was done and the amount paid without the usual credit of 60 days. From the very liberal and satisfactory manner in which this loss has been arranged we feel great pleasure in recommending the "Franklin Insurance Company" to those wishing themselves really protected against the dangers of the destructive element – water and fire. J. P. Dobyns, Esq. of Maysville, is the agent. R. & E. W. Taylor, of Millersburg, Ky, Oct 12, 1844

Grand Whig Rally, at Dover Ky, October 23rd, 1844. At Dover, Ky. October 23rd, 1844. "Union for the sake of the Union," H. A. Wise's toast from Clay's speech, "Our Country – our whole country. Do unto all Nations, as you would wish they should do unto you." Henry Clay.... Friends to the best interest of your country of every party, denomination and sex, come to our meeting, you will have a hearty welcome and good cheer. "Come and let us reason this matter together." Hons. Thomas Corwin, John J. Crittenden and Gen. Thomas Metcalfe, were personally spoken to at the Ripley meeting, we confidently expect two of them, at least to be present. Other distinguished Whigs are invited and expected to attend, from Indiana, Ohio, Pennsylvania and Kentucky A. Soward, J. J.

The Maysville Eagle

Anderson, A. Fox, C.A. Lyon, W. B. Johnston, L. Tabb, committee of Arrangements

Death, Died in this county, on the 11th inst. At his uncle's David Lindsey, William W. Parker, in the 18th year of his age.

In Lancaster, Ky, on the 22nd of July last, Stephen T. Mason, Esq. in the 27th year of his age. The deceased was a gentleman of the highest order of intellect, and had he been permitted to live a few years longer, would no doubt have risen to distinction. He possessed a heart overflowing with the milk of human kindness, and his premature death was deeply lamented by a large circle of admiring friends. H.

Extract of Logwood, Shoe brushed, castor oil, jujube paste, cider Vinegar, at the sign of the Golden Mortar, Market Streets, M.F. Adamson

Strayed. A copy of "Pencilling's by the Way" has found its way out of our counting room. Will the borrower please return it immediately and save the expense of a copy? A. M. January & Son, Maysville, Oct. 16, 1844

Post Note, Taken up as a stray, by Watson P. Diltz, of Bracken County, living one and a half miles above the town of Augusta, on the Ohio River, a bay house, about fourteen hands, one inch high, about five years old, with a scar on his near shoulder, supposed to be the effect of the wind fistula. No other brands or marks perceivable. Appraised to 25 dollars. Given under my hand as a justice of the peace for said county, this 24th June 1844. Solomon Taylor, J. P. Oct. 16, 1844

Last & cheapest. Prices Reduced at the Big 6. in consequence of the extensive arrivals of new goods at the Big 6, and the heavy stock now in store, we are determined to close out at greatly reduced prices, to make room for more... Let the public bear in mind that the Big 6 is the only cheap store in the place, and that our goods will be put at such prices that cannot be competed with. Country merchants will do well to call and examine our stock, and prices. We shall have a full stock in store during the season and open new goods weekly. E.M. Sell & Co. Proprietors of Big 6, Market Street. Maysville, Ky. Oct 16, '44

Commissioner's Sale. By virtue of several decrees of the Mason Circuit Court, rendered at the August term, 1844, in the suits of Marshall & Penn, against Mary Levi and Mordicai Levi, John and Thomas Salisbury against the same, two suits of John Allen against the same, and Vincent Crab

The Maysville Eagle

against the same. The undersigned commissioner appointed by said decrees, will sell at public auction at the court house door in Washington, on Monday, the 11th day of November being Circuit Court day a tract of land containing one hundred and forty five acres, lying near the town of Minerva, in Mason County. Also several town lots in the city of Maysville, or so much of said land and town lots, as shall be sufficient to satisfy said decrees. The sale will be upon a credit of twelve months, and the purchasers will be required to give bonds with good security, payable to the complainants in the order mentioned above. The said bonds to have the force and effect of sale or replevin bonds taken under Execution, and shall bear interest from the date. Jas. M'Millin, Com'r. October 12, 1844

Removal. The subscriber has removed to his large three story brick ware house, on the corner of Wall and Second streets, one square below January & Son, & Cutter & Gray. His house is large and convenient, and he is determined to offer to farmers and merchants, every possible inducement, to deal with him, as he will take every kind of produce that he can dispose of and will be liberal as to prices and offers all the facilities in the articles of groceries, in his line. He also will keep constantly on hand the most approved quality of Kanawha Salt. He has also a lot attached to his salt shed, where all wagons have the privilege, of standing all night, free of charge. Thankful for the patronage he has heretofore received, he hopes to merit a continuance of the support of his old friends and customers and by diligent attention to add many new customers to his list. John B. McIlvain. Maysville, Oct 12, 1844

Cash for Hides. We will pay the highest market price for beef hides, green or dry, delivered at our drug store. Seaton & Sharpe, Maysville, Oct. 9, 1844

As Cheap as Any!! We have sold, are selling, and will continue to sell dry goods as cheap as any house in the county, at the sign of the "cheap cash store," in Washington. Our assortment is composed of the latest and most fashionable styles and patterns, just received from the East. Terms, cheap for cash, equally cheap on short time to punctual customers. John Lashbrooke, Henry W. Wood, Washington, Oct. 9, 1844

Administrator's Sale, of personal property. The undersigned as administrator of the estate of Samuel H. Culbertson, deceased, will expose to sale, at public auction, on Tuesday the 15th instant, on the corner of Second and Sutton Street. Maysville, the personal property belonging to his estate as follows: Dry goods, hardware, chairs and bedsteads, the

The Maysville Eagle

running gear of a four horse wagon, cooking and wood stoves & c & c& c Sale to commence at 9o'clock, a.m. on that day and continue from day to day until all is sold. Terms all sums under $5 cash in hand, on sums above that, six months credit, with approved security. Milton Culbertson, Adm'r. Maysville, Oct. 5, 1841

Fall and Winter Dry goods, by W. & C. Fellowes & Co. Auction, Jobbing & Commission Merchants, Louisville, Kentucky very long list of articles.

Candle Factory. The subscriber would respectfully inform the Merchants, Grocers, and citizens of Maysville and vicinity, that he has commenced the manufacture of candles in this place, and is now prepared to furnish them with as good an article of candles as can be obtained in Cincinnati or any other place, and upon the same terms. The undersigned hopes from his long and practical experience in the business, that he will merit and receive the patronage of the citizens. John Ford. N. B. Candles will be exchanged at all times for tallow and soap grease; and orders from a distance remitting the amount required will be promptly filled. Maysville, Sept. 18, 1844

I will barter for domestic linseys, flannels, jeans, linens, socks, and all descriptions of goods of home manufacture. I have received my stock of fall and winter goods, which is equal to any in the city. Jos. F. Brodrick. Nov. 18, Market St. Maysville, Oct 2, '44

Thomas Y. Payne, informs his clients that during his absence, attending court on the circuit for the next six weeks. Mr. Henry Wadsworth will remain in his office and attend to the bringing or preparation of suits. In cases where it is desired personally to consult him he expects to be in his office each Saturday. Maysville, Sept. 28

New and Cheap Goods. S. Shockley is receiving and opening a general assortment of fall and winter goods, which have been purchased in Philadelphia upon the most favorable terms and will be sold low for cash... long list of clothing articles. Maysville, Oct 5, 1844

Piano at Auction. Will be sold at Public Auction on Thursday, the 17th October at Peter Jones' cabinet Ware room on Second Street, Maysville, A Piano Forte, persons wishing to purchase can examine the Piano before the day of sale. A. A. Wadsworth, Maysville, Oct. 12, 1844

Exerts from Whig Meeting. At a Whig meeting held in Flat Rock, Bourbon Co., Ky. Oct 1844 Thos. W. Shepherd was chosen President, and James

The Maysville Eagle

Squires Secretary. A free barbecue on the farm of Jos. Wilson, near Flat Rock on the 30th inst. And that Peter Branlet, H. A. Rogers, Samuel Hedges, Jas Squires, Dr. Guisenburg, Jos. Wilson Douglas, Lewis & B. F. Rogers, be a corresponding committee, specially to invite such orators and statesmen, as in their judgment are best calculated to present a full and fair exposition of those principles and measures. ... invite the Clay Clubs of this and the adjoining counties, the Paris and Mountsterling Brass Bands, the Paris and Carlisle Glee Clubs, and extend such other invitations as in their judgment is proper. Resolved; that Turner Fisher, Warren B. Rogers, French Simpson, Willoughby Scott, Samuel O. Wilson, Shelton Bradley, H. A. Rogers, Peter Bramlet, Voluey Higgins, Miner S. Hibler, John Hedges, Harvey Letton, W. M. McKim, Jacob Sodusky, E. J. Smith, Labon Letton, John Hutchcraft, Douglas Lewis, Volney Lindsay, John S. Morgan and Hiram Norton, of Nicholas; M. Q. Ashby and Capt. Wm. Markham of Bath, Gen. Samuel Williams and Enoch Smith, of Montgomery by a committee to solicit subscriptions to said barbecue, as see that they be furnished (sufficient for ten thousand person) on the premises; the meats by 2o'clock on, the evening of 29th, and the bread & c. by 9 o'clock next morning..... Resolved, that Aquiea Roeby, Peter Couchman, H. A. Rogers, Joseph Watkins, Robert Kilgore, Joseph Furgerson, James Squires, Joseph Wilson, John B. Smith, Samuel Donovan, W. S. Rogers, Wm. Richart., Peter Bramlet, Fielder Letton and Crawford Terry, be a committee of arrangement, whose duty it shall be to attend to providing plank for tables and stands and to the preparation of the dinner & c. Resolved that Will. Collins and Geo. R. Foster, be appointed marshals of the day, and that they be requested to appear in full uniform, and that French Simpson, Charles Porter, Hiram Norton, Shelton Bradley, Jeremiah Terry, Samuel Hedges, Miner S. Hibler, Edward Stone, and Nathaniel P. Rogers, be requested to act as Assistant Marshals and that they were on the occasion some insignia of Office. That the Marshals & Committees be authorized and requested to prohibit intoxicating spirits of all kinds from being brought on the barbecue field...... Thos. W. Shepherd, Pres. James Squires, Sec

A Whig of 1776 and of 1844. Correspondence of the Albany Evening Journal. Mr. Editor, Sir: There is a piece in your paper which contains a mistake I wish to rectify and at the same time give some other information. I was born in the year 1764,. In my 12 year, when the British landed in Boston, I lived sixty miles from Boston, in Rhode Island, and know all about the war in that quarter. My father moved to Vermont, when I was fifteen years old. When Bennington battle was fought, I was out all night. I helped to move Burgoyne off to Boston. In those times it was Whig and Tory. My father was a Whig and all my brothers, and I have maintained the

The Maysville Eagle

glorious principles ever since. I lived in the war, and went to Casdeton a soldier, and was a minute man two years. The mistake I refer to is the statement that I live near Akron, Ohio; it should be Akron in the state of New York. I have seven sons and three sons – in – law, and one hundred and twenty descendants in the whole and out of them thirty three voters, all Whigs, who will vote for Clay. Stephen Bates.

Virginia Moving – The last Lynchburg Virginian says that Fielding Jones, Esq., of that county has renounced Locofocosim, and that one of the Vice Presidents at the Whig Convention held at Buckingham Springs a few days ago. Dr. Binford of Buckingham, has also abandoned the Locofoco party….. The last Fincastle "Valley Whig" contains a card signed by eight of the citizens of Botetourt to wit: John Goode, James McNeil, Morris Hickkok, Anthony Rhodes, Simeon Fitch, Fielding Stuart, Jubal Waldron and Henry M. Johnson, renouncing Locofocosim…. The last Charlottesville Advocate contains a card from Robert Simpson, Esq. (who recently heard and "eloquent and convincing speech from V. W. Southall") renouncing locofocosim.

This issue contains many articles that involve political issues that lead up to the Civil War. Anyone interested in researching the causes of the Civil War should read these articles.

The Augusta Female Academy. The winter term of the Augusta Female Academy will open on Monday the 14th Oct. under the care and tuition of Mr. W. G. Hathaway and Lady, both experienced and successful teachers. The trustees of this institution feel assured that its real merits and advantages need only be known to the public, to secure for it a liberal amount of patronage. The location of Augusta is known to all, as beautiful and healthy. It is easy to access, being on the river, 45 miles above Cincinnati, and 10 miles below Maysville. The society of the place is cultivated, intelligent, and moral. It is the seat of a flourishing institution for the education of males and many parents who were educating their sons in Augusta College, have learned to appreciate the important advantage of placing their daughters where they could bare the attention and care of a brother. The most scrupulous regard will be had to the deportment and welfare of the pupils whose parents do not reside in town. Young ladies from abroad can be accommodated with board, on moderate terms in the family of the Principals, or in respectable families in the vicinity of the Academy. The terms of tuition are the same as heretofore. For the common Eng. Branches, $12 per term, 5 months. For the younger classes, $8. high do including any of the modern languages and if desired Latin and

The Maysville Eagle

Greek $16 per term. For Drawing paining music and other ornamental branches, extra charges will be made proportioned to the tie devoted to them In behalf of the Trustees. S. G. Shropshire, Sec'y Augusta, Sept 23, 1844

New Store. Worthington & Anderson are just receiving and now opening at No. 12 Market Street, Maysville, Ky. In the house recently occupied by Jos. F. Brodrick, an entire new stock of foreign & Domestic dry goods. Maysville, Sept. 18, 1844

Maysville, Saturday December 27, 1845

A large portion of our columns today is occupied with the speech of Mr. M'Clung, and the correspondence on the subject of the removal of the county seat of Mason. Mr. Waller, it will seem, in accordance with his pledges during the canvass, feels himself bound to vote for the removal of the county seat to Maysville....Mr. Breeden occupies the same position. Col. Key, our worthy senator, in his response to the communication from Maysville avows his opinions frankly and candidly.....

Samuel Hatfield, Esq., has been elected a Representative to the Kentucky Legislature for Simpson County, in place of Alfred M. Williams, deceased.

We are authorized to announce Messrs. Thos. Y. Payne, Nat. Poyntz and R. H. Stanton as candidates for the city council, in the Middle Ward at the ensuing election.\

Lengthy letter dated December 25, 1845 Maysville, written by H. Waller, Messers. H. Taylor, Joseph Forman and Isaiah ? about the removal of the county seat.

Letter dated December 24th 1845 to Col. Marshall Key signed Wm. Mackey, Nat. Poyntz, R. G. Dobyns, Stephen Lee, James Artus, Rich'd Collins, H. T. Pearce, A. A. Wadsworth, A. M. January, Sam'l K. Sharpe, F. T. Hord, Jno. M. Duke, Thos. Y. Payne, R. H. Stanton about the removal of the county seat.
A reply by Marshall Key.

New Years Ball. It is hoped that our friends throughout the county will all attend the Ball. They shall receive a cordial welcome, and we promise our best exertions to make the affair creditable to the city and pleasant to those

The Maysville Eagle

who attend. The managers and young men who propose attending it are requested to meet at the Mayor's office on Monday 29th proximo.

Rev. Wm. H. Lawder of the Methodist Episcopal Church, will preach in the Methodist Church, on tomorrow at the usual hours, it being his regular appointment.

Married, in Maysville, on Tuesday evening by the Rev. R. C. Ricketts, Mr. Charles Sandford to Miss Mary M'Chord.
In this city on Thursday evening, by the same, Mr. James Purtee, to Miss Mary Ellen Phillips.

On Thursday evening the 25th inst. By Rev. R. C. Grundy, in the immediate vicinity of Maysville, Mr. Habel Haslam to Miss Lavina Cooper.

Near Mr. Carmel on the morning of the 23rd inst., by the Rev. John A. Clarke, Capt. W.D. Coryell of Mason to Miss Emily D. O'Bannon of Fleming County.

Deaths. In Lewis County, Ky. On the 29th inst. Of the dropsical affection, Mr. William Strode, formerly of Mason county, in the 48th year of his age. He was a devoted member of the Methodist Church, and bore his long affliction with humble submission to the divine will. His death was calm, but triumphant.

Notice. The partnership heretofore existing between us, under the style of Thomas & Henry is this day dissolved by mutual consent, except so far as relates to the settling up of our business. We earnestly request those who know themselves to be in debt to us to call and settle, either by cash or note. Those having claims against us please present them. O. H. P. Thomas, John Henry. Dec. 27, 1845

D. S. Hudson Watch Manufactureer. Maysville, Dec. 27, 1845

Christmas and New Year Presents at the Eagle Book Store.

We Nurse Wanted. I wish to obtain the services of a wet nurse, and will pay good wages provided I can get one immediately. R. C. Grundy. December 23rd, 1845

The Maysville Eagle

Dental Surgery. H. Marshall respectfully announces to the citizens of Maysville and vicinity, his intention to establish himself in his profession in this city. His long experience and application to his profession enables him to say with confidence, that any of the various operations in dental surgery will be preformed according to the best principles and latest improvements of the science. Teeth inserted with an exact resemblance to nature, on pivot or on plate, with clasps or by atmospheric pressure, so that they will answer all the ordinary purposes of mastication. Toothache and all local diseases of the mouth cured, and the mouth restored to a healthy condition. Children's teeth regulated and brought into their proper places. All operations insured to answer the purpose intended. Call from the country or surrounding villages promptly responded to. H. M. desires to rely upon his workmanship and his uniform deportment to establish a reputation among the citizens of Maysville. Should references be desired, however, as to character or profession skill, they can be given in abundance. Until a suitable office can be obtained he will be happy to wait on any who desire his services, at Mrs. A. W. Coburn's on Third street or at their dwellings. Reference – Dr. Shackleford, Maysville, Dec 23, 1845

For Hire, a first rate servant woman, from first of January next, for the ensuing year. A. M. January & Son. Maysville, Dec 23, 1845

Stray Cow, was taken up as a stray by James A. Keith, of Mason County, living near Beasley's Creek Meeting House, a red cow, with a white face and a white streak along the back, no marks. Supposed to be about 6 or 7 years old. Appraised to $10. Given under my hand, as a Justice of the Peace for said county, this 15th day of December 1845. Jesse Turner, J. P.

Close of the Year. Received two day since, by express from Philadelphia, a few patternus black watered, watered and striped silks, super mode colored thibet shawls, plain black mouslin de lande, gloves, vails & c. Kirk and Fant.

City Election. The annual election for Mayor and Councilmen will be held in this city on the 1st Monday in January next, as follows, to wit: In the upper ward at O. M. Weeden's office, J. W. Johnson, O. M. Weeden, and W.E. Seddon, inspectors. In the Middle Ward at the city hall, Elijah Johnson, Henry Tureman, and H L. Davis, inspectors. In the Lower Ward, at the office of Davis & Daulton, D. Carrel, O.H. Davis and Charles Phister, Inspectors. James A. Lee, City Clerk. Dec. 8th 1845

The Maysville Eagle

Notice The annual election for president and directors of the Maysville Insurance Company, for the ensuing year, will be held at the office of said company on Monday, the 7th day of January next, between the hours of 10 o'clock a.m. and 12m. Cks. B. Ryan, Sec'y Dec. 13

"Sign of the Saw" Axes! Axes!! 40 boxes of Hartford Collins, Simmons and Beatt's manufacture, for sale at the hardware house of N. D. Hunter, No. 20 Front St. Dec. 6

Take Notice. This is to forewarn all persons from trading for a note that I gave to John Kemper some time last summer, for $35 due the 25th day of December, 1845, as I am determined not to pay it, as it was fraudulently obtained. James Laytham. December 23rd 1845.

Hemp. I am paying cash for good dew-rotted hemp. Jno. P. Dobyns. December 20, 1845

Rye Flour, fresh ground and for sale at the Mill of Jno. D. & Wm. Stillwell, Maysville, Dec 2nd

E. M. Sell & Co. Positively but 20 days more in Maysville, call and see at what discount goods will be sold. Maysville, Nov. 25

Was committed to the jail of Mason County, Ky., on the 15th instant, three Negro Boys- Berry, Frank and Caleb. Berry is 18 years old, 5 feet 4 inches high – black. He had on a brown janes coat and pants and round crown white hat – says he belongs to Peter Campbell of Tazewell County, Va. Caleb is 16 or 18 years old, 5 feet 9 inches high – black. Had on a brown janes coat, flax linen pants and black wool hat – says he belongs to Peter Edwards of Madison Co. Ky. Frank is 30 or 35 years old, 5 feet 7 inches high; had on a brown janes coat and pants and fur cap – says he belongs to Silas Newland, of Madison Co Ky. John Hill. Jailer, Sept 20, 1845

Runaways in Jail. There are now confined to the jail of Greenup County, Ky. Two Negro Men supposed to be runaways. One of them calls himself Peter the other Littleton. Peter is about 22 years of age, very black, about 5 feet 8 inches high, and of genteel appearance and has a pleasing countenance when spoken to. He had on when committed, a pair of blue jeans pantaloons, a coarse cotton shirt and a woolen cap He is partially ruptured and wears a truss; he says he belongs to Thomas Moffitt, of Rockbridge county, Virginia. Littleton is about 6 feet high, about 25 years of age, very black. Had on when committed a blue cloth dress coat, an old

The Maysville Eagle

black fur hat. He says he belongs to John Hagin of Lancaster County, South Carolina. Allen Myers, Jailor of G. C. December 24, 1845

By Arrivals from the East. Ely D. Anderson, No. 11, Front Street, has just received a large and general and complete assortment of Fall and Winter Dry Goods & c. & c.

Doctor Rogers, Compound of Syrup of Liverwort and Tar .. for consumption of the lungs, spitting of blood, coughs, colds, asthma, pain in the side, bronchitis & c. Which has performed such remarkable cures in the city of Cincinnati, curing cases that the first physicians had given up to die. The original certificates of which the following extracts are taken, can be seen at the agents store. Mr. Hirma Plummer, who resides on Main street between 8th and 9th street Cincinnati Ohio, states that his wife was cured of a most inveterate case of consumption by this syrup. She had been lingering for two years in the care of two Cincinnati medical men, one of whom finally gave her up to die. She used this syrup, however and is now well. Mr. Jesse B. Dorman, who resided on 7th street, corner of church alley between Walnut and Vine streets, Cincinnati, Ohio, one of the oldest and most respectable citizens in this place says: that he was so far gone with a most distressful asthma of 30 years standing, that his friends gave him up to die, but was immediately relieved by the use of this medicine. Mr. Justice Finch states that his lungs were diseased to such a degree that he was constantly spitting blood, had a most dreadful hacking cough, continually breaking his rest and continued to get worse, though in the care of an able physician. The case was arrested and cured by the use of a little less than three bottles of this medicine. From the Hon. Judge Wm. Burke, Cincinnati, Ohio. He informs the public that the statements of Mr. J. Finch, with respect to this medicine are, are entitled to their implicit confidence, and that he can fully corroborate what has been said from his own experience, having used the medicine himself with the most decided benefit, and he consider it valuable. The wife of Rev. Geo. W. Malay, City Missionary and pastor in charge of Maley Chapel, Cincinnati Ohio, says that after having tried various preparations for the disease for her lungs, without getting any relief, until a friend advised a trial of Dr. Rogers' Syrup, a few bottles of which cured her immediately. Available medicines are kept constantly on hand and for sale in Maysville, Ky. by Seaton & Sharp, Agents, December 13, 1845

New Fancy Goods & C. Just received a great variety of rich, and low price vases; mantle ornaments; tea bells, table mats......No. 9 Main Street, below third opposite Trust Company Bank, Cincinnati. Wm. S. Sampson.

The Maysville Eagle

Sign of the Pad Lock, No 10. Market Street Maysville, Ky. Keep constantly on hand a general assortment of building hardware, viz: know locks, latches, bolts, butts and screws; also, carpenter tools of every description, such as planes, chisels, hand axes, hatchets, compasses, rules, saws & c., & c., besides all other goods belonging to their branches of business, which they will sell as low as can be purchased in the Western country. Coburn & Reeder. December 2, 1845

Notice. We are preparing to start east about the first of January and respectfully urge those who are indebted to us, by note or book account, to come forward and furnish the needful to pay our debts and buy a new stock of boots and shoes. Miner & Cruttenden, Maysville, Dec. 9 1845

Sale of Negroes. By virtue of a decree of the Mason Circuit Court, rendered at the late November Term, in the Chancery Suit of George Mefford's Adm'r and al vs. Thos. T. G. Warren and al, I shall sell at public auction, in front of the Court House in Washington on the 1st day of January next, six valuable slaves, belonging to the estate of said George Mefford, dec'd. Terms make known on the day of sale. Edw'd Waller, Com'r. Dec 15, 1845

Wholesale Crockery & Glass Ware. The subscriber has on hand a large stock of common printed and fancy goods adapted to the country trade, which will be re-packed to order, at the lowest market price. Also, an extensive assortment of Boston an Pittsburgh Glass Ware at factory prices. Wm. S. Sampson, No. 32 Main St. below 3rd, opposite T.C. Bank, Cincinnati. Nov. 29

Just received, 5 hnds, New Sugar, also rice, raisings and Virginia Tobacco, for sale by Artus & Metcalfe, Dec 4, 1845

New Style Dress Goods & c. & c., Kirk & Fant have just received some beautiful cashmere and mouslen del lanes, styles entirely new; rich black and blue black, watered and figured silks; cashmere and thibet shawls, new style bonnet and cap ribbons, gloves and mitts, a great variety, thread lanes, edging & c. To which they invite attention. In a few days they expect to be in receipt of their entire stock of fall goods, and will be able to offer inducements, in style quality and prices, to all who may favor them with a call. Maysville, Sept. 20, 1845

The Maysville Eagle

Long's Panacea and Perfective healer. It is not avarice that induces the subscriber to offer to the public his "perfective healer," but through the suggestions of numerous friends, who have been relieved of affliction by it, and his own disposition to contribute as much as he can to the relief of the sufferings of his fellow creatures. Those who know the valuable efficacy of the Panacea have influenced him to make its virtues known and to disseminate it throughout the country; it is not only palliative and astringent but will effectually heal and cure the following diseases, viz: Sctophalous Affections, Chronic Ulcers.... As to burns and scalds it heals as if by a charm. It is the least trouble and the most ancient remedy for the above named diseases of anything now before the public. Dover, Ky., Nov 27, '44. E. Long. The following are among the numerous certificates, now in possession of the proprietor, showing the great efficacy of this valuable medicine. This is to certify that I have used in my family, on divers occasion, Long's Panacea and Perfective Healer, and believe that it saved my wife's breast from the knife of the Surgeon and perhaps her life, as the doctors who saw it pronounced it incurable. The relief was immediate and permanent. Given under my hand this 19th October , '44. Benjamin Ogdon. Mason County, Ky. I, William T. Craig, of Mason County, Ky. Do certify that I have used Long's Panacea and Perfective Healer in my family, and believe that it is the most efficient remedy for burns, of anything extant, and indeed as he says "it heals as if by a charm." W. T. Craig. I do hereby certify that I have used in my family for many years, Long's Panacea and perfective healer, and believe it is a most efficient remedy, and preferable to any I have ever used in all fresh wounds, burns, scalds, bruises, sprains, & c. and for such, can cheerfully recommend it. Dan'l Runyon. Minerva, Oct 1844 I do hereby certify that I was afflicted with the Piles for several years, and found nothing that would give me relief until I used Long's Panacea & Perfective Healer, which has, I believe, made a perfect cure of my case. Joseph Cushman. Dover, Ky, Jan 8th 1844. For sale wholesale and retail by Seaton & Sharpe, general agents, Maysville, Ky.

Dr. M. F. Adamson, takes this method to inform his friends and the public, that he does not intend leaving this city, (as some have been busy circulating,) but will continue the practice of medicine and attend strictly to its duties. His office is on Sutton Street, nearly opposite the Lee House,, where he can be found during the day and at night at his lodgings at Mrs. Goddard's. Maysville, August 23, 1845

Union Hall to Rent. This splendid house will be finished and ready for a tenant in thirty days, is located on the most desirable spot in the city of

The Maysville Eagle

Maysville for such an establishment; its external appearance is inviting, while it internal arrangements are unsurpassed in the west for comfort and convenience. This desirable house is now offered for rent, on such terms as to insure a handsome profit to a person qualified for hotel keeping. There is nearly fifty rooms in this house, a full portion suitable for parlors. The increase of building in Maysville, the last two years, is greater than for seven years preceding. None need apply but such as have a character as Hotel Keeper. Address the subscriber, post paid, Maysville, Ky. Wm. Mackey. Maysville, Sept. 24, 1845

Eight Hundred Dollars Reward. Ranaway from the subscriber living in Fayette County, Ky., on Sunday night, the 18th instant, three Negroes, a man, woman and child. The man is about 25 years of age, dark complected, slow in speech, and has a down look when spoken to, he is about 5 feet 6 or 7 inches high. The woman is about 23 years old, bright mulatto, her hair rather long, she is somewhat delicate in appearance. The child is about 7 years old, a bright mulatto boy. The above reward will be given if taken out of the state and secured in any jail so that I may get them; $400 if taken in any county in Ky, except Fayette,$50 will be given if taken in Fayette County, and all reasonable expenses paid. Ben. McCann. July 30, 1846

Planters Tobacco Warehouse, the subscriber begs leave to inform the tobacco planters of Mason and the adjoining counties, that he has again located in this city, and is now having erected, on the corner of Second and Wall streets, opposite the warehouse of Mr. John B. McIlvaine, an extensive brick tobacco warehouse, for the purpose of receiving and prizing Mason county segar-tobacco, which will be completed in time for the growing crop, and where at all times, the highest market price will be paid for the article. For the benefit and convenience of such farmers as may wish to engage next season in the cultivation of the cegar leaf, he has made arrangements that enable him to furnish them gratis, with the pure see, and also printed direction, touching not only the cultivation but the particular management of the crop, that is always necessary in order to secure the farmers the highest prices. Having been engaged for the last sixteen years in this county, not only in the manufacture, prizing and shipping, but also the raising of the article of tobacco, he flatters himself that his experiences in every department of the business will enable him to give every satisfaction to the persons abroad who may desire to make investments in the justly celebrated Mason County Tobacco; and to such he would respectfully tender his services and pledges himself to give his close

The Maysville Eagle
and undivided attention in the selection, purchase prizing and shipment of the Tobacco. William B. Mooklar. Maysville, Sept. 24, 1845

Kentucky Collegiate Institute. We do not hesitate to say, that is our opinion, this institute, in the experience of its Principle, the extent of its apparatus, and its invited number of pupils, combines advantages and facilities for improvement, both to males and females, not met with in any other Literary Institution in the West; and that its merits are justly appreciated by an intelligent community may be inferred from the fact, that its list of pupils has been complete, and we have been compelled to reject several applications at the commencement of every session since its organization. The next session will commence the first of October next and close the first August. A few pupils may be received for the next year, if application be made in season, as we are limited to 20 males and a few females – but no pupil will be admitted, either as a boarder or resident scholar, for a less term than the full collegiate year. Terms, for boarding tuition, washing, fuel and lights $150.00 H. Maltby, A.M. Principal. Flemingsburg, June 28, 1845 References. Rev. Dr. John C. Young, Danville, Ky. N. D. Coleman, Esq., Vicksburg, Miss. , Rev. N. H. Hall, Lexington, Ky. B.C.Adams and I. Maltby, Esq. New Orleans, La. Rev. N. L. Rice, D.D., Cincinnati, Ohio. Lewis Collins, Esq. Maysville, Ky. Tho's Holladay, Esq., Blue Licks, Ky.

Bullock's progressive Power Press, For hemp, tobacco, hay, cotton, oil & c. This press is now offered to the public with entire confidence on the part of the inventor. It has been subjected to the severest test and trials, for three years to prove its practicability, its power and durability. Hundreds have been put in use and without a single exception, have not only answered the expectations of the inventor, but are highly valued by the purchasers to five time the cost……. The subscriber is the owner of nearly all of the territory bordering on the Ohio and Mississippi Rivers, and he would respectfully say to the people of Maysville and its vicinity that he has come amongst them for the purpose of introducing his press – he can be found at all times by enquiring at the drug store of Seaton & Sharp, where he will be pleased to see all who may call, and exhibit tot hem a press in operation. He would likewise say that he is prepared to sell presses, and also to sell territory, in small or large quantities, as it may please the purchaser. Daniel Goss. Maysville, September 17, 1845

Spikes and Heavy Wrought Nails. Just received a lot of spikes and heavy wrought nails, not usually kept in this market. For sale at the iron store of Jno. H. Richeson. Nov. 13th 1845

The Maysville Eagle

New Iron Establishment. The undersigned having lately purchased of A. M. January & Son in this city, their stock of Iron and Nails, has opened in the warehouse formerly occupied by Jno. B. McIlvain, on Sutton Street, an establishment for the sale of Juniata iron and nails, manufactured at the fligo works, Pittsburgh, and warranted to be superior to any other brands brought to this market. Also a general assortment of German, English and American steel of the most approved brands. I invite my friends wishing any thing in the line to call and examine the stock – it will be constantly kept complete in the various sizes of iron – receiving additions regularly as required from the above manufactory. To the old customers of Messrs. A.M. January and Son, the undersigned would say that his best exertions shall be used to promote their interest in making purchases of Iron and hopes they will so find it as to give him their patronage. I will be pleased to see them at the new stand. The business of the house will be conducted similar to that lately pursued by A. M. January & Son. Jno. H. Richeson. Maysville, July 1, 1845

Having disposed of our entire stock of iron and steel to Mr. Jno. H. Richeson, and not intending to keep for sale any of those articles hereafter, we take much pleasure in recommending our customers and others to call on Mr. Richeson for their supplies – they will find his assortment of iron, steel and nails, very fine, both in assortment and quality. They will also find Mr. Richeson industrious, polite and attentive and every way worthy the confidence of all those ... January & Son.

Washington Livery Stable. Corbin Gallaher, Informs the public that he has erected a large and commodious livery stable in Washington on Main Street, nearly opposite the Post Office and is prepared to keep horses at very moderate terms. He has likewise c.. y.. hand horses, buggies, barouches & c for hire. Washington, Ky. Jan. 8, 1845

Farm for sale. Lylburn Farm in Greenup County is now offered for sale. This land is very valuable to any one who will occupy it, as there are three furnaces within three miles of it, and all the fresh, hay and stock of every kind finds a ready market at the furnaces and at better prices than any market in the interior of Kentucky. About 100acres cleared bottom land under fence and now in corn, 25 acres bottom land just cleared; it represents many inducements as it is one of the bets locations to raise cattle, the mountain range being very fine. The farm lies on Little Sandy River, one and a half miles from Greenupsburgh. The terms will be liberal. I would sell the stock, farming tools & c., with the land and 500 to 1000

The Maysville Eagle

bushels of corn. I will exchange it for town property in Maysville or land in Mason County. John B. McIlvain. Maysville, May 7, 1845

Lee House. Mrs. Judith Goddard respectfully announces to the public that she has removed to the large and splendid hotel recently erected on the corner of front and Sutton streets. Which she has fitted up in a style of elegance and comfort unsurpassed by any similar establishment in the state. She solicits continuance of public patronage. Maysville, Feb 12, 1845

Consumption of the lungs, liver complaint asthma, bronchitis, pains or weakness of the breast, chronic coughs, difficulty of breathing, spitting of blood, and all affections of the pulmonary organs......Wistar's Balsam of Wild Cherry.... From Dr. Baker, Springfield, Washington Co., Ky. Messrs. Sanford & par; Springfield Ky. May 14, 1845 Gents – I take this opportunity of informing you of a most remarkable cure performed upon me by the use of Dr. Wistar's Balsam of Wild Cherry. In the year of 1840 I was taken with an inflammation of the bowels, which I labored under for six weeks, when I gradually recovered. In the fall of 1841 I was attacked with a severe cold, which seated itself upon my lungs and for the space of three years I was confined to my bed. I tried all kinds of medicines and every variety of medical aid without benefit, and thus I wearied along until the winter of 1844 when I heard of Wistar's Balsam of Wild Cherry. My friends persuaded me to give it a trial, though I had given up all hopes of recovery, and had prepared myself for the change of another world. Through their solicitations I was induced to make use of the genuine Wistar's Balsam of Wild Cherry. The effect was truly astonishing. After five years affliction, pain and suffering, and after having spent four or five hundred dollars to no purpose, and the best and most respectable physicians had proved unavailing, I was soon restored to entire health by the blessing of God and the use of Dr. Wistar's Balsam of Wild Cherry. I am now enjoying good health and such is my altered appearance that I am no longer known when I meet my old acquaintances. I have gained rapidly in weight, and my flesh is firm and solid. I can now eat as much as any person and my food seems to agree with me. I have eaten more during the last six months than I had eaten five years before. Considering my cure almost a miracle, I deem it necessary for the good of the afflicted and a duty I owe to the proprietor and my fellow men (who should know where relief may be had) to make this statement public. May the blessings of God rest upon the proprietors of so valuable a medicine as Wistar's Balsam of Wild Cherry. Wm. H. Baker. Price $1 per bottle. Sold in Cincinnati on the corner of Fourth and Walnut streets, by Sanford & Park. Gen'l Agents

The Maysville Eagle
for the western states. Sold in Maysville by Seaton & Sharpe and in Carlisle Ky by W. W. Fritts & Co. October 18, 1845

New Wholesale and Retail Hardware House. Coburn & Reeder are now receiving and opening at their store house on Market street in Maysville, two doors south of the wholesale dry goods house of L.C. & H. T. Pearce, a large and general stock of hardware, consisting of all descriptions of cutlery, mechanics' tools, building hardware, saddlery and other articles belonging to their branch of merchandise. Their goods have been purchased within the last thirty days in New York and Philadelphia and principally of importers, manufacturers and their agents, at unusually low prices for cash. They therefore confidently invite merchants, mechanics farmers and all others to call and examine their stock. The public will not long remain in doubt of either their willingness or ability to sell hardware at wholesale or retail, for cash, or on short credit to punctual customers as cheap as it can be purchased at any market in the western country. Experience is knowledge – call and prove the sincerity of our offer, Maysville, October 11, 1845

New Goods, we have commenced receiving our fall and winter stock of dry goods and in a few days will be in receipt of our entire fall purchase. We would be pleased to see our old customers and to have a call from the public generally, as we can offer strong inducements to those wishing to purchase, both in regard to prices and elegant styles of French and English fancy goods. Our stock of domestic goods is also large and complete which we will sell at the lowest cash prices. Rees & Allen. Maysville, Oct 1st 1845

Fire Life and Marine Insurance. The Lexington Insurance Company, continue to insure fire, life and marine risks and pay all losses, sixty days after proof of loss. The rates of insurance as low as other offices. Apply to Artus & Metcalfe, agents Maysville, January 24, 1844

10 cases thick boots, 5 cases kip boots of Cincinnati manufacture and a very superior article for sale low by E. R. Perry, Market Street

Birmingham Hardware....Also fine steel fire setts and standards, swivel percussion gun locks, white metal ten and table spoons, tinn'd mullers .....for sale. Tyler Davidson & Co. No. 106 Main Street 3 doors above Com. Bank, Cincinnati, Nov 8, 1843

The Maysville Eagle

Hemp! Hemp! The undersigned will pay the highest price I cash, for water rotted and good well cleaned bright dew or snow rotted hemp, delivered a the new warehouse on Fourth above limestone street. N. Arthur, agent Maysville, August 16, 1845

Maysville and Cincinnati Packet. The splendid and fast running U. S. Mail steamer Clipper, Jno. F. Ballenger, Master, will leave Maysville on Tuesdays, Thursdays and Saturdays at 9 o'clock, a.m. and Cincinnati on Mondays, Wednesday s and Fridays at 10 o'clock a.m. Shippers may rely upon her punctuality as she has been purchased expressly for the trade and will be continued in it. October 15, 1845

Family Flour, for sale at our mill low for cash and not inferior to any sold in the market. Jno. D. & Wm. Stillwell. Maysville, July 23, 1845

Steam Engine for sale. I have for sale a steam engine with 11 inch cylinder, 3 ½ foot stroke, with two boilers, 41 inches in diameter, and double 15 inch flues. It may be seen at any time in operation at my cotton mill, and can be delivered to the purchaser by the 1st of November. Richard Henry Lee. Maysville, Sept. 20, 1845

Sleeper. At this manufactory No 3 East Fifth Street, opposite the Dennision House, has constantly on hand a large and general assortment of Silk, Gingham and cotton umbrellas, and a splendid assortment of flounced, fringed, scollop'd and plain edged parasols, parasoletts and sun shades. Wholesale and retail at Eastern prices. Cincinnati, June 11, 1845

Behold the Good Samaritan! And the Golden Morter, No. 11, Market Street, Maysville, Kentucky. Where all kinds of drugs, medicines, paints, oils, dyed stuffs, glass, varnishes, spices, ink, vinegar, paper, blacking, starch, segars, tobacco, instruments, bandages, glue, turpentine, matches, soaps, garden seeds, syringes. ...... Physicians, Merchants, and grocery houses will find it to their advantage to call and examine if they don't buy there will be no charge for showing goods, by J. W. Johnston & Son. Nov. 22, 1845

Hathaway's Patent Cooking Stove. I have made an arrangement with Mr. Joel Kirk.... ...... stove, by which I shall be enabled to keep a constant supply of all sizes of them on hand, with any kind of trimmings that may be wanted. The castings of these stoves are heavy and thicker than any ever offered for sale in this market. This stove stands so low that the boilers when full can be put on and taken off of them with ease; the oven is large

The Maysville Eagle

and commodious, and will bake and roast to perfection; the flame of the fire plays direct on all of the bottoms of the boilers, and boils or steams quick at every point, and consumes as little fuel as any other stove now in use. There is nothing complicated about this stove, but every part of it is plain and perfectly easy to manage. The unparalleled reception of these stoves in the Eastern cities, during the last year, renders it worthy the inspection of all interested in promoting the comfort and convenience of those engaged in the labor and drudgery of the kitchen. The subscriber having had a good opportunity of seeing them fully tested, does not hesitate in all sales to warrant them to please the purchasers. It after giving the stove a fair trial, they are not pleased with it; if returned to me without damage, except what occurs in using them on trial, I will refund the payment of the same on demand. John C. Reed. No. 17, Market Street, Maysville. Feburary 24, 1844 References may be had, concerning the Hathaway Stove by calling on the following gentlemen who have them in use. George Cox, John Armstrong, Dr. M F. Adamson, Eli F. Metcalfe, Dr J. Shackleford, C. Shultz, F.W. Cleaney, Oliver Anderson, all of Maysville. E. H Herdon, Jonston Ross, Hugh McIlvain, all of Mayslick, J. J. Key, Capt. Montjoy, H. G. Musick, James McMillen, Thos. H. White, all of Washington. William Metcalfe, Flemingsburg and John Fleming, West of Washington.

Rope Walk for Rent. We would rent our rope walk for one year or for a term of years, if desired by any one who may with to rent. It is situated at the lower end of the city of Maysville, the most eligible in the county- it is of good length and located immediately on the bank of the Ohio River.. Terms Favorable. January & Huston, Maysville Feb. 26, 1845

Thomas Y. Payne, Attorney & Counsellor at Law, Maysville, Kentucky. Will practice in the courts of Mason and the adjoiing counties and in the court of appeals. Office on Front Street, two doors above Rees & Allen's Dry goods Store. July 27, 1844

Light! Light!! The subscriber at his establishment known as "the Lower Pork House" has commenced the manufacture and will hereafter keep on hand a supply of summer stearine candles, not inferior to any made by the best manufacturers in Cincinnati or elsewhere. He also continues to manufacture a superior article of lard oil, with which in connection with the candles, he believe can be produced as much and as good light, from a given quantity as can be produced by any concern in the west. He invites attention to these articles and solicits a continuance of patronage. Wm. B. Alvord. Maysville, April 16, 1845

The Maysville Eagle

Fine! Fine!! Fine!!! John T. Johnson of Lynchburgh, Va. Has sent us five boxes of his celebrated chewing tobacco, as a specimen. He wishes to introduce his Tobacco in this market, and has authorized us to sell it at a less price than he is getting for it in the Eastern markets. We invite those wishing a fine article to call and examine it. Thomas & Henry. P. S. We have also in store fifty boxes and kegs tobacco, to other brands comprising all the various qualities usually sold in this market; all of which we offer for sale at very low prices. Oct. 15

Wheat Wanted. We are paying the highest price in cash for wheat. J. D. & W. Stillwell. Maysville, July 23, 1845

Ch's W. Franklin. Richard C. Ricketts, Wholesale Grocery, Produce, Commission and Forwarding House. Franklin & Ricketts, Maysville, Ky. The undersigned would respectfully inform their friends and the public generally, that they have this day formed a co-partnership, in this city, under the style of Franklin & Ricketts, for the purpose of transacting a general Grocery, produce, Commission and forwarding business. In the large, convenient and fireproof warehouse on second street, two doors below the corner warehouse of Messrs. Cutter & Gray, where they intend keeping a regular assortment of select groceries, which they offer as cheap for cash, or hemp bacon and lard, as any offered in the market. They are also prepared to receive and forward merchandize to purchase, bale, store and ship hemp, with quick dispatch and on liberal terms. The business of the firm will be under the care and attention of Mr. Franklin, who from his long experience and the strict personal attention which will be given, flatters himself that he will be able to give entire satisfaction in selecting hemp and produce on orders from abroad, and thereby recur to the firm a share of the business concentrated in this city. Cha's W. Franklin, Richard C. Ricketts. N. B. A lot choice fresh flour, of Dayton Mill, for family use, on hand and will be kept constantly for sale by F & R .Maysville. April 16, 1845

Henry Waller, Attorney & Counsellor at Law. Maysville Will practice in the courts of Mason and the adjoining counties and in the court of appeals. Office the same occupied by Payne & Waller on Main Cross Street. July 27, 1844

Maysville. Saturday January 10, 1846

The Maysville Eagle

This is the season for settling accounts generally, and as those to whom we are indebted need their money and expect payment, we earnestly request our friends and patrons who are indebted to this establishment, to recollect that our ability to pay depends upon them altogether. If they are prompt, we can be so; if they are negligent and tardy, our credit must of necessity suffer. The amount of each individual indebted to us is small, but the aggregate is large and of pressing importance to us. Persons at a distance will greatly oblige us by remitting the sums due by mail, at our risk and expense.

We tender our thanks to Col. Key, of the Senate and Messrs. Waller and Breeden of the house of representatives for their politeness in forwarding us important documents.

Fatal Affray, a reencounter tooplace at Bayou Sara, on Saturday the 27th inst, between Nelson Swain and Joshua Turner, in which Turner was killed with a knife. Swain was arrested and committed for trial.

The late rise has broken up the ice as far as Pittsburgh, and as soon as it disappears, the navigation of the River will be unobstructed from Pittsburgh to New Orleans. Boats from above arrived this morning.

The bill to divorce Mrs. S. C. P. Thomas from her husband, Ex-Governor Thomas, of Md., and restore her to her original name of Miss S. C. P. M'Dowell, has passed the Virginia House of Delegates by a unanimous vote.

Abijah Fisk, one of the most eminent merchants of N. Orleans, died in that city recently.

For the Maysville Eagle. Mr. Collins By permission I send you for the Eagle, the following beautiful and appropriated lines addressed to the signers of the Washingtonian Pledge. They are from the pen of a lady whose poetic talent and zeal in the temperance cause both entitle them to a place in our paper and to a careful perusal by all who have a taste for poetry or regard for the temperance cause. The authoress first wrote them at the request of her Sunday scholars, and hearing that they may be peculiarly applicable to some of the Mason County Washingtonians, as well as elsewhere, she now submits them to the press hopping that they may be a salutary warning to some, and productive of good to many. Happy are we if we have no such Temptress in our city, as is described in these beautiful lines. Happy would it be for the world and most happy for the temperance

The Maysville Eagle

cause did none such exist in the community at large. May the tie soon come when a wholesome public sentiment shall make it impossible for a male and much more a female to violate the temperance pledge with impunity. R. C. Grundy. The poem follows, but is partly obscured.

Religious Notices. The Rev. Dr. Edwards of Boston will preach in the Presbyterian Church on to-morrow morning, on the rights and privileges of the men in regard to the Sabbath. At night, in the same house, Dr. Edwards will address the citizens on Temperance – and as he has been very appropriately styled the Apostle of Temperance in the United States, a very large audience will no doubt attend to hear him.

The Rev. Mr. Grubbs will preach at the Baptist Church to-morrow, at the usual hours.

To all who it may concern: Gentlemen who owe the estate of A. W. Bascom, dec'd and whose notes and accounts are due, will please have the kindness to call upon H. Gray or S. D. Lillitson, immediately and make payment. The condition of the estate warrants us in making this request, and we hope our good friends will comply. At the same time we ask leave to remind the old friends of the late A. W. Bascom and the public generally, that the jewelry business is still conducted, as heretofore, at the same place, under the supervision of the Trustees, where a complete stock of jewelry is kept constantly on hand and offered for sale at reduced prices, and where watches & c. can be repaired at short notice in the best manner. Our thanks are due for past favors and we respectfully solicit a continuance. T. K. Ricketts, J. Shackleford, H. Gray, Trustees. Maysville, Jan. 10, 1846

Servant Wanted. A liberal price will be paid for a servant woman during the present year, who is well acquainted with washing, ironing and house work, enquire at the Eagle Book Store, Maysville, Jan 3, 1846

Female Collegiate Institute, Georgetown, Ky. T. F Johnson, A. M. Principal with five associates. The 15th Session will open March 1st and close July 17th, 1846 after a public examination of three days. Terms in advance. Board and tuition, $80.00, Music, with use of instruments, $25.00, French, Drawing or Painting, $10.00, Vocal, Music or Embroidery, $ 3.00. No extra charge for use of library and philosophical apparatus Pupils who practice their music at the institute, will be charge for extra fuel. January 1, 1846. Frankfort Com.

The Maysville Eagle

Committed to the Ja'l of Fleming county, Ky., on the 16th day of October 1845, by George W. M'Cord, Esq. a Negro Man calling his name "Isaiah," about 45 or 50 years of age. 5 feet 8 inches high, dark copper color, has a scar on his left wrist, about 2 ½ inches long, he says he belongs to John Gaither, near Lexington. Ky. He states that he was hired at a hemp factory in Lexington, from which he escaped. The owner of said slave is requested to come forward, prove property and pay charges, otherwise he will be disposed of according to law. A. W. Rock. Jailor of Fleming County, January 7, 1846

New and Fresh Arrivals of Watches & Jewelry from the East. I have just received a splendid assortment of watches, Jewelry & c. which I will sell low for cash. J. S. Gilpin, Jan 6, 1846\

Dr. Jos. Taylor, Dentist, Would respectfully request those indebted to him to come forward and settle their accounts. As this is the first public call which he has made, he hopes that it will be attended to promptly. Maysville, Dec 20, 1845

To My Debtors. All persons owing me will please come forward and settle as early as possible, as I am preparing to go east for a new Stock of goods and need the funds to pay my debts. Jos, F. Brodrick. Maysville, January 3, 1846

Crockery, Glass and China Wares, Selected expressly for the country trade. The subscriber has now on hand a complete assortment of printed, fancy, china, and glass wares of new style, which together with his stock of common ware, will make the assortment equal to any in the market,, and can hardly fail to give satisfaction to those who are desirous of purchasing. Country merchants and others wishing to purchase are respectfully requested to call and examine the stock at No 92, main street, between 3rd and Lower Market streets, corner of Hopple;s Alley, Cincinnati. Wm. S. Sampson, Dec 30, 1845

Boyd House for Sale. This desirable property in the town of Concord, Lewis County, Ky. Is now offered for sale. Its fine location off the banks of the Ohio River, immediately opposite a good stream boat landing at all seasons of the year., with a good grade from the house to the river, renders its situation most desirable. The main house is 60 feet front and 24 feet deep; immediately in the rear of the house is a first rate kitchen, dining room and smoke house, with a garden of excellent fruit trees and shrubbery. The house has been newly painted and is in excellent repair. It has all the

The Maysville Eagle

conveniences for a public house, the stable and corn house recently built, is large and commodious and conveniently situated. Attached to the house is also an eligible and well known store room and a first rate stand for selling goods. I have occupied the above property as a public house and store room for some 10 or 12 years. On the adjoining lot and immediately opposite the grade is two rooms suitable for a grocery and boat store, a good stand for both, as there is two wool yeads at this place and a first rate country for all kinds of produce. On the same lot is another room, also on front suitable for a tailor, saddler or shoemaker's shop. In front of all the above property is a number of fine shade trees. Also on the same street a lot 66 feet front, 132 feet deep with a stable and under good fence. Also a brick house, two stories high on Main Street with a first rate cellar under the house, and is suitable for a family residence. Concord is as healthy a situation as there is in the west with a fine country back and on the opposite side of the River. The market is well supplied with every description of produce. It has the facility of a daily line of steam packets to Cincinnati and Portsmouth, being 30 miles from the latter place and 20 miles above Maysville. The celebrated Esculapia Springs is only 12 miles distant and this is decidedly the best landing place above Maysville..... All the above property is very valuable and I am determined to sell at a great bargain, separate or all together, to suit purchasers. I deem it unnecessary to say any more, as those wishing to purchase would like to examine the property, which will recommend itself. For any other information I refer you to Mr. Wm. Buck Parker, at the Franklin House and James A. Lee, Esq., Maysville. Ky. John L. Boyd Concord, Dec 16, 1845

Cincinnati Bell and Brass Foundry. The undersigned will furnish bells of all sizes of superior quality, for churches, public buildings, steamboats & c which he will warrant for clear richness brilliancy of tone and durability, cannot be equaled by any manufacturer elsewhere in the west, and at the lowest prices. Geo. L. Hanks. Columbia Street, east of Ludlow, Dec. 16, 1844

List of Letters, remaining in the Post Office at Flemingsburg, Ky. January 1st 1846, which if not taken out in three months will be sent to the general post office as dead letters. John D. Arnold, William Browning, Robert Bell, Sarah? Bell or E. Mark, James Burns, S. Botts, William S. Botts, Miss R. C. Barnes, Dixon Clack 2, David Culberson, Walter Chandler, Presley Oliver, Clerk of Circuit Court 2, Elizabeth L. Coburn, Basil Crookshanks, R. B. Craver, W. H. Darnall, George W. Demit, William M. Evans, John Feemster, Casander Fitzgerald, William Farrow, Boyl Gill, William Green, Jefferson Harrow, Mrs. Howe, John D. Howe, Lewis Hanes, W. N.

The Maysville Eagle

Harrison, Zacariah Johnson, Benjamin F. Lalshhaw, Dr. George G. Lowry, Thomas Morrow, John S. Morgan, Dr. J. B. Moffett, George Marshall, George H. Marshall, John N. Procter 2, James Pickerel, E. S. Pepper, Rev. W. W. Patton, William Phillips, Robert Payne, James C. Plank, Jas Ross, Sec'y Fleming Lodge 2, George Sanders, Sr. , Benjamin Saunders, Amos Sutton , Joshua Wier, David M. Williams, James P. Wilson, Wm. Walker, J. J. Wyatt, H. L. Yateman. Those calling for letters will say advert'sed. Jan 3, 1846. John G. Payne, P.M.

New Goods, R. Collins has received his fall and winter assortment of goods, consisting of a general variety of fancy & staple goods. Hats, shoes, boots and fresh importation of bolting cloths, from No. 0 to No. 10. All which he offers wholesale and retail at greatly reduced prices, and invites purchasers to examine his stock. Front Street, Maysville, Oct. 11, 1845

Adams
  B. C., 113
  G. Adams & Co., 27
  Sumrall & Adams, 3, 34
  William, Dr., 33
Adamson
  Dr. M. F., 111
  M. A., 96
  M. F., 100, 118
Adlum
  Major, 29
Alexander
  Elijah, 16
  James, 50
Allen
  James, 10
  John, 100
  Rees & Allen, 90, 116, 118
Alvord
  Wm. B., 118
Anderson
  Anderson & Sharpe, 84
  Ely D., 95, 109
  G.W., 44
  Ira, 30
  J. J., 98, 100
  Jno. W., 18
  John W., 23, 33
  Kirk, Anderson & Sharpe, 78
  Oliver, 118
  Worthington & Anderson, 105
Applegate
  Richard, 41
Armstrong
  Armstrong & Collins, 94
  Debora, 41
  Dorsey & Armstrong, 83
  John, 16, 118
  Johnston, 20, 27, 40
Arnold
  John D., 123
Arthur
  N., 117
Artus
  Artus & Metcalfe, 73, 110, 116
  James, 23, 27, 54, 105
Ashby
  M. Q., 103
Aston
  A.M., Mrs., 41
Atkinson
  William, 27
Augusta Female Academy, 104
Avard
  S. Doctor, 51
Bacon
  Jacob, 53
  John G., 41
Bailes
  Frances, 28
  John, 28
  William, 28
Baker
  Dr., 115
  Hiram, 56
  Wm. H., 115
Baldwin
  Eliz. J., Mrs., 41
  Garrison, 25, 33, 41
  Samuel, 18
Baley
  Warren, 27
Ballard
  A.E., 1
Ballenger
  Jno. F., 117
  Wilis, 46
Baltzell
  James, 71
  Thos. W., 71
Baly
  William, 27
Barabino
  Madam, 71
Barclay
  Dorcus, 15
  William, 15
Barker
  E.B., 32
Barnes
  R.C., Miss, 123
Barr
  Enoch, 15
  Robert S., 15
Bartley
  John, 41
Bascom
  A. W., 90, 121
  Nolin & Bascom, 80
Bassett
  David, 56
Bates
  Stephen, 104
Battle of Bradywine, 87
Baxter
  John, 26
Bayles
  Benjamin, 45
  Benjamin, Maj., 41
Bayless
  B., 46
Beagley
  Mrs., 98
Beall
  Samuel T., 20
Beatty
  A., 31, 44, 73, 96
  Adam, 19, 20, 41
  Judge, 30
  W. R., 68

The Maysville Eagle

William R., 64, 65
Wm., 41
Wm. R, 62
Bell
  Robert, 123
  Sarah?, 123
Bender
  Dorothy, 37
  Elizabeth, 37
Berry
  A., 63
  George W., 41
  James, 41
Berryman
  J.S., 23
Best
  J., 31
Beverley
  Carter, 29
Bickley
  Mr., 89
  William, 88
  Wm., Maj., 98
Bigelow
  Zeikel, 52
Binder
  Elizabeth, 37
Binford
  Dr., 104
Binns
  John, 36, 39
Blacksmith, 87
Blaetterman
  G. W., 82
Blaine
  S. L. & Co., 76
Blair
  Lydia, Mrs., 41
Blanchard
  Robert T., 89
Bland
  John, 41
Bledsoe
  Capt., 43
Blythe
  Dr., 21

Bodens
  Col., 29
Bodley
  Wm. S., 7, 19
Bogle
  William, 46
Bolinger
  Henry, 51
Boon
  Mr., 28
Boone
  Edward, 41
  Jacob, 22
  William, 22
Botts
  George W., 3
  S., 123
  William S., 123
Boud
  Samuel, 1
Boulton
  Rice, 28
Bowman
  A.B., Col., 43
Boyd
  John L., 123
  Stephen, 41
Boyd House, 122
Boyls
  William, 41
Bradley
  Shelton, 103
Bragg
  Thomas, 64
Bramlet
  Peter, 103
Branlet
  Peter, 103
Brasher
  P.C., 41
Brawner
  Ignatius, 41
Breckenridge
  John, Hon, 71
  John, Rev. Dr., 71
  Ste. T., 41

Breeden
  Mr., 105, 120
Brent
  Hugh J., 93
  Thomas Y., 79
Brewer
  Asahel, 42
  Edward, 41
  William, 41
Brodrick
  J. F., 69
  James, 53
  Jos. F., 96, 102, 105, 122
  Messrs. Pearce, Fant & Brodrick, 83
  Pearce, Fant and Brodrick., 68
Brodrick's Mill, 50
Brotherton
  Col., 21
Brown
  George, 41
  H. B., 92
  John, 64
  Mary, 3
  Mr., 98
Browning
  Hord & Browning, 42
  William, 123
Brownlee
  James J., 2
Bryan
  Phineas S., 41
Buchanan
  Andrew, 69
  Maxwell & Buchanan, 69
  R., 53, 60
  Robert, 69
Buckner
  Phillip, 18
Budd
  Joseph, 41
Buel

The Maysville Eagle

Judge, 14
Buford
  William, 10
Bull
  E. H., 22
Bullock
  J.W., 31
  James W., 20, 41
  Lewis, 19
  William, 43
Burden
  Samuel, 10
Burgess
  A. G., Dr., 76
  J., 32
  Mr., 23, 33
  Phil'n, Capt., 46
Burgoyne
  Evan T., 62
Burke
  Wm., Hon Judge, 109
Burkitt
  John, 78
Burns
  James, 123
Burroughs
  Richard C., 46
Burrow
  John, 71
Bush
  James M., 46
Butcher
  M'Laughlin, 97
Byers
  James, Capt., 20, 32, 41
  Wm., 41
Cahil
  Oliver, 41
Caldwell
  Captain, 86
Calhoun
  Mr., 55
Calvert
  George S., 30
  W.M., 57

Campbell
  Evin, 41
  Grant & Campbell, 5
  Mr., 24, 47
Carpenter
  P., 49, 60
  William, 41
Carrel
  D., 107
Carrell
  D., 75
  Mrs., 8
Carrothers
  Mr., 10
Carter
  R. S., 93
  Wm. T., 38
Cartmill
  Andrew, 27
Catlett
  David, 41
  Elizabeth, Miss, 41
Cavan
  John A., 58
Chalfant
  James, 41
Chambers
  F. T., 90
  F.T., 58
  Hannah, 46
  J. S., 52, 64
  J.S., 57
  John, 20, 61
  John J., 93
  John, Hon, 93
  W., 52, 57, 64
Chandler
  Walter, 123
Chaplin
  Moses M., 29
Cherry
  Elijah, 86
Chew
  John, 41
Chiles

David, Gen., 46
Chinn
  Geo., 46
Cincinnati Bell and Brass Foundry, 123
Clack
  Dixon, 123
Clark
  Mary, Mrs., 41
  Septimus D., 32
  Thomas C., 26
Clarke
  Chas., 97
  Clarke & Ryan, 58
  Gen., 1
  John A., Rev., 106
  John M., 83
  Mr., 56
  Septimus D., 46
  Thomas, 34
  Thomas C., 10
Clarke & Ryan, 47
Clay
  Mr., 43, 44
Cleaney
  Cleaney & Shultz, 59
  F.W., 118
Clendenen
  George W., 23
Clift
  Benjamin, 18
  Wilson, 25
Cloud
  Rev. C.W., 43
Coburn
  A. W., Mrs., 107
Coburn & Reeder, 110, 116
Coburn & Stockwell, 60
  Dr., 9, 47
  Elizabeth, 123

The Maysville Eagle

Cockenhover
  Jacob, 46
Coe
  John, 41
Cohen
  Alfred, 72
Cole
  N. L., 97
Coleman
  J. C., 71
  N. D., 113
Collins
  Agnes A., Mrs., 41
  Armstrong & Collins, 94
  Edmund, 18
  George & co., 80
  George & Co., 71
  George W., 41
  James, 1
  L., 67
  Lewis, 20, 113
  Mr., 2, 98, 120
  R., 124
  R.A., 1
  Richard, 66, 83, 92
  Rich'd, 105
  Will, 103
Coniers
  Isaac, 27
Conn
  Col., 31
  James, Col., 41
Conwell
  William P., 95
Cook
  William B., 20
Cooke
  Alicia, Miss, 41
Cooper
  Lavina, 106
Copper
  Hugh, 41
Corbin
  Jeremiah, 27
Coreman
  John B., 44
Corwin
  Thomas, 99
Corwine
  Amos, 5
  Geo., 5
  George, 41
Coryell
  W. D., Capt., 106
Coryvell
  W. D., Capt., 98
Couchman
  Peter, 103
Cowgill
  John, 20, 41
Cox
  E., 59, 67, 71
  Edward, 5, 8, 48, 66, 91
  George, 5, 118
  L.M., 95
  Mrs., Oliver W., 70
  Oliver W., 70
Crab
  Vincent, 100
Craig
  Mrs., 60
  S.W., 31
  Whitfield, 28
  William T., 111
Craver
  R. B., 123
Crittenden
  John J., 99
  Sally, 46
Crocket
  John, 27
Crookshanks
  Abram, 41
  Basil, 123
Crosby
  Mr., 9
  O & S., 9
Cruttenden
  Miner & Cruttenden, 110
Culberson
  David, 123
Culbertson, 68
  John, 26
  Milton, 102
  Samuel H., 101
Cummins
  Henry B., 58
Curtis
  Marshall, 66
Cushman
  Joseph, 111
Cutter
  Cutter & Gray, 101
  Henry, 80, 85
  Henry & Co., 68
  Mr., 61
Darnall
  W. H., 123
Daulton
  Davis & Daulton, 107
Davidson
  Tyler, 116
Davis
  Benjamin, 41
  David, 88
  Davis & Daulton, 107
  H. L., 107
  H. N., 83
  Jacob, 46
  James C., 49
  John, 30
  John D., 83
  John N., 41
  Joseph, 41
  Nathan, 49, 61
  O. H., 86, 107
  Thomas, Dr., 2
  Davis & Hanson, 28
Dayton
  R.A., 65

The Maysville Eagle

Dement
  Richard, 5
Demit
  George W., 123
Dennis
  Nicholas, 41
Dennision House, 117
Derrett
  Wm. B., 41
Desha
  Ex-Governor, 55
  Joseph, Gov., 46
Dewees
  J.C., 7, 46
Dewein
  V., 73
Dickerson
  Hughart & Dickerson, 83
Diltz
  Watson P., 100
Dimmitt
  N. S., 95
Dixson
  Archibald, 17
Dobyns
  Ann, 16
  Berry, 23
  Edward, 16
  J. P., 74, 99
  Jno. P., 108
  Leach & Dobyns, 67, 80
  Leroy, 34
  R. G., 105
  R.G. & Co., 58
Dodson
  Mr., 66
Dollis
  Isaac, 41
Donelly
  Captain, 39
Donovan
  Samuel, 103
  T. M., 71
Dorman
  Jesse B., 109
Dorr
  Jona. Dr., 9
Dorsey
  Dorsey & Armstrong, 83
Dougherty
  Alexander, 6, 25
  Charles, 41
  Milton, 79
  Thos. M., 7, 25
Douglas
  Jos. Wilson, 103
Douthet
  Robert, 24
Downing
  J., Major, 52
Drake
  Cornelius, 80
  Jacob, 25
  W. H., 79
Driskell
  Peter, 72
Dudley
  John, 59
Dudley Hotel, 49
Duell
  Elizabeth, Miss, 41
Duke
  Basil, Dr., 98
  Dr., 49
  Jno. M., 71, 105
Dunbar
  G. Dr., 61
Duncan
  Joseph, 46
  Walter, 46
Dunhar
  G., Doctor, 47
Dunn
  Walter, 45
  Wm., 31
Duponceau
  Peter S., 55
Durbin
  Daniel, 24
Durret
  House of Durret & Co., 50
Durrett
  Paul, 46
  W.B., 31
Duzan
  Abraham, 41
  John, 41
Dye
  Granville H., 76
  John, Sen., 45
  Mary, 45
  Richard, 41
Dysart
  Isaac G., 65
Eagle Book Store, 47, 51, 53, 69, 92, 106, 121
Eagle Bookstore, 91
Eagle office, 73
Eagle Tavern, 23, 59
Easthem
  Wm., 44
Easton
  James, 41
Eddy
  Jonas, 71
Edgar
  John T., 21
  John T., Rev, 20
Editor, 69
Edwards
  John, 46
  John, Col., 12
  Rev. Dr., 121
Ely
  Jacob W. H., 46
Ernest
  Tolbert, 48
Etherington
  Min, Mrs., 41
Evans
  John H., 70
  Thomas L., 93
  William M., 123
Evens

G. W., Surgeon
   Dentist, 47
   Jefferson, 32
Fairfield
   Sumner Lincoln, 86
Fant
   Kirk & Fant, 94, 110
   Kirk & Fant., 90
   Kirk and Fant, 107
   Messrs. Pearce, Fant & Brodrick, 83
   Pearce, Fant and Brodrick., 68
   R. C., 69
   Wm. O, 75
Farrow
   William, 74, 123
Feemster
   John, 123
Fellowes
   C., 102
   W & C., 75
   W., 102
Female Collegiate Institute, 121
Ficklen
   William, 82
Ficklin
   Daniel, 98
   James K., 86
Fielder
   Stark, Col., 45
Fields
   Thomas J., 95
Fiffe
   Perry, 46
Finch
   Justice, 109
   Susan, 88
Fisher
   Turner, 103
Fisk
   Abijah, 120

The Maysville Eagle
Fitch
   Simeon, 104
Fitzgerald
   Casander, 123
Fleming
   John, 118
   William P., 20
Foley
   Jas G., 77
Ford
   Charles, 3
   John, 102
Foreman
   Thomas M., 79
Forman
   E., 50, 57
   Ezekial, 48
   Geo., 52
   George L., 50
   J. S., 50, 57
   Jno. S., 69
   John S., 85
   Joseph, 105
   Thomas, 79
   Thos., 52
   Tho's., 96
   Thos. S., 48
Foster
   Geo. R., 103
   Nat., 77
Fowler
   John, Capt., 43
Fox, 100
   Arthur, 46
   Thos. H., 30
Franklin
   Ch's W., 119
   Dr., 45
   Mary, 46
Fritts
   W. W., 116
Frizzel
   Archibald, 63
   H., 65
Furber
   John N., 94
Furgerson

   Joseph, 103
Gaither
   John, 122
Gallaher
   Corbin, 114
Gates
   Mr., 43
   William, 30
   Wm., jr., 31
   Wm., Sen., 31
Gaylord
   Gaylord & Co., 60
   Gaylord & Co, 47, 54
Gibson
   John B., 65
Gifford
   Samuel, 46
Gilbert
   Nathan, 41
   William, 41
Gill
   Boyl, 123
   Erasmus, 46
   Presley, 4
Gillaspie
   Tavern, 10
Gilpin
   J. S., 57, 122
Given
   Benjamin, 63
Glasscock
   Thomas, 72
Glendennin
   John, 10
Goddard
   Judith, 59, 115
   Mrs., 47, 59, 111
Goin
   Antoine, 46
Goode
   John, 104
Goodwin
   Libins, 45
Goss
   Daniel, 113

Graham
  Henry, Capt., 24
Grant
  Peter, 20, 27
  Robert, 23
Grant & Campbell, 5
Granville, 67
Gray
  Cutter & Gray, 101
  H., 121
  Hamilton, 85
Green
  H. E., 1
  Henry, 50, 53
  John, 46
  Mrs., 51
  Robert C., 65
  Taylor & Green, 51
  Taylor & Green, 74
  William, 123
Grover
  Thomas, 41
Groves
  Edward, 46
Grubbs
  Rev. Mr., 121
Grundy
  R. C., 106, 121
  R. C., Rev., 106
Guisenburg
  Dr., 103
Gully
  Shelton, 91
Hagin
  John, 109
Hale
  Thomas, 46
Hall
  Gilbert, 41
  J. S., 86
  John, Capt., 41
  N. H., Rev., 113
  W., 20
Ham

Sarah, Mrs., 41
Hamilton
  Mr., 24
Hampton
  Wade, 65
Hand
  H., 66
  Hawkins, 62
  Mr., 66
Hanes
  Lewis, 123
Hanigan
  E.B., 46
Hanks
  Geo. L., 123
Hannegan
  E.B., 32
Hanson
  J., 28
Hardy
  James G., 20
Harl
  Baldwin, 72
Harman
  Smith & Harman, 81
Harris
  Ebenezer, 9
Harrison
  Alvira, 93
  Dominick, 97
  Peter, 97
  W. N., 124
  William H., 65
Harrover
  Alexander, 41
Harrow
  Jefferson, 123
Hart
  George, 65
  Leander, 30
Hatfield
  Samuel, 105
Haweis
  John, 28
Hawkin
  Mill, 95

Hawkins
  A.F., 44
Hayden
  William, 41
Hayne
  Robert Y., Gen., 55
Healy
  John, 39
Heath
  Nathan, 62
Hedges
  John, 103
  Samuel, 103
Helm
  Merideth, 3
  Samuel, 3
  Thomas, 3
  William, 3
Henderson
  Mathew H., 65
Hendrickson
  William, 17
Henrie House, 89
Henry
  J. W., Dr., 47
  John, 106
  Thomas & Henry, 119
  Wm., 46
Herbst
  Geo., 71
Herdon
  E.H., 118
Hibler
  Miner S., 103
Hickey
  Judge, 43
Hickkok
  Morris, 104
Hieatt
  Mr., 29
  S., 31
Hiett
  Isabella, Miss, 41
Higgins
  Richard, 43

The Maysville Eagle

Voluey, 103
Hill
  John, 108
Hixon
  N & N, 40
Hixson
  Messers., 42
Hixson, Morton &
  Hixson, 8
Hoage
  A., 65
Hoblitzell
  Dennis B., 4, 41
Hockaday
  John, 24, 28
Hodge
  Samuel, 27
  William, 53
Hoffman
  Margaret, 37
Holiday
  John, 93
Holladay
  Tho's, 113
Holland
  George H., 48
Holley
  Nancy, Mrs., 41
  Stephen, 41
Hollinback
  Law. Van, 41
Holton
  Benjamin F., 1
  James H., 23
Hord
  F. T., 68, 105
  F.T., 51
  Francis T., 20, 46, 57, 84
  Mr., 43
Hord & Browning, 42
Houghton
  Elizabeth, 46
Housley
  Nancy, Mrs., 41
Howard

The Maysville Eagle
Dr., 44
Howe
  Elizabeth, 65
  John D., 123
  Melvina, 65
  Mrs., 123
Howorth
  George, 37
  John, 37
Hudnut
  Joseph H., 5, 23
Hudson
  D. S., 91
Hughart
  Hughart & Dickerson, 83
Hukill
  Nathan, 41
Hull
  Amos G., 61
Humphreys
  Charles, 3
Hunt
  William, 80
Hunter
  N. D., 74, 98, 108
  N. D. & Co., 67
Huston
  Felix, 86
  January & Huston, 8, 25, 47, 52, 58, 118
  William, 66
  William, Jr., 20
Hutchcraft
  John, 103
Hutchins
  Morris A., 66, 95
Hutchinson
  James E., 81
  Randall, 65
Hutchison
  Israel P., 65
Iles
  Washington, 27

Indians, 1
Irving
  Washington, 46
Isrel
  Mary Ann, Miss, 41
J. W. Johnston & Co, 47, 52
Jack
  J. P., 87
  John, 5
Jackson
  Andrew, 29
  Cutter & Jackson, 80
  David, Jr., 80
  Mr., 61
  R.G., 23
  Thomas, 20
Jacobs
  Benjam N, 60
  Edler Lewis, 93
  J., 27, 60
  James, 60
  L., 27, 60
  Lewis, 60
  Lewis Jacobs & Co, 60
January
  & Son, 101
  A. M., 81, 100, 105
  A. M. & Son, 67, 69
  A. M. & Sons, 67
  A. M. January & Son, 107, 114
  A. M., & Son, 85
  A.M., 21, 83
  Andrew M., 20
  January & Huston, 58, 118
  Peter, 41
  Peter T., 43
  Samuel, 21
  Wm. H., 81

The Maysville Eagle

January & Huston,
  8, 25, 47, 48, 52
January & Son., 114
Jenkins
  Daniel, 4
  Overton, 4
John
  John, 6
Johns
  Maria, Miss, 41
Johnson
  Benj., 46
  E., 71
  Elijah, 107
  Henry M., 104
  J. P., 87
  J. W., 64, 107
  John T., 119
  Mrs., 87
  T. F., 121
  Zacariah, 124
Johnston
  E.P., 75
  J. S., Hon., 44
  J. W., 47, 48, 52,
    61, 69, 70, 84
  J. W. & Co., 58
  J. W. & Son, 117
  John, Dr., 44
  Judge, 44
  W. B., 100
  W.B., Dr., 31
Jones
  Fielding, 104
  George W., 77
  Jones &
    Rammelsberg,
    95
  P. B., 71
  P.B., 41
  Peter, 102
Jos
  Gillespie, 41
Justice
  Moses, 41
Kane
  George, 36

Keim
  Daniel M., 55
Keith
  James A., 107
  John A., 65
Kelly
  John, 21
  Kelly's Cash
    Store, 81
  P. H., 81
Kemper
  John, 108
Kendal
  Rebecca, Mrs.,
    41
Kenton
  John, 24
Kentucky Collegiate
  Institute, 113
Kerlin
  William, 41
Kerr
  Thomas, 41
Key
  Col., 105, 120
  Harriet, 46
  Isham, 46
  J.J., 118
  Marshall, 15
  Marshall, Col.,
    45, 105
Kilgore
  Robert, 103
Kirk
  & Fant, 94
  Kirk & Fant, 110
  Kirk and Fant,
    107
  Kirk, Anderson &
    Sharpe, 78
Kirk...
  Joel, 117
Knight
  Nelson, 46
Knowsley
  Washington, 23
Kothe

Jno. W., 22
Lacy
  Walter, 46
Lalshhaw
  Benjamin F., 124
Lamb
  Lucinda, Mrs., 41
Lambs
  John, 42
Lamby
  Mrs., 46
Landrum
  Fran. Rev., 46
Langhorne
  Capt., 5, 22
  Capt. M., 8
  E. B., 71
  John T., 59
  Maurice, 18
  R. J., 63
  R.J., 63
Langley
  Mr., 41
Lashbrooke
  Hannah Jane, 88
  John, 101
  W. & Sons, 67
Lavender
  John, 65
Lawder
  Wm. H., Rev.,
    106
Lawson
  John, 28
Laytham
  James, 108
Leach
  Leach & Dobyns,
    67, 80
  Rev. Dr., 20
Lee
  Charles, 46
  James A., 92,
    107, 123
  R. H., 50, *56*, 57,
    94

Ric'd Henry, 66, 83
Richard Henry, 8, 117
Richard R., 20
Stephen Col., 54
Stephen Lee, 105
Stephen, Capt., 22
Stephen, Col., 98
Lee House, 115
Leftwich
  Aug., 44
Letcher
  Governor, 86
Letton
  Fielder, 103
  Harvey, 103
  Labon, 103
Levi
  Mary, 100
  Mordicai, 100
Lewis
  Douglas, 103
  Isaac, 33, 41, 53, 78
  M. G., 46
Lewisburg Factory, 78
Light
  Rev., 92
Lillitson
  S. D., 121
Lindsay
  D., 6
  Volney, 103
Lindsey
  David, 100
Linthicum
  Charles, 56
  Joshua, 34
Litefoot
  James, 41
Logan
  Benjamin, Col., 1
Lokey
  Willaim, 62

The Maysville Eagle

Long
  Col., 44
  E., 111
Lowry
  George G., Dr., 124
Lylburn Farm, 114
Lynn
  James, 72
Lyon
  C. A., 100
  John, 10
M'Cann
  Arthur G., 46
M'Cauley
  John, 41
M'Chord
  Mary, 106
M'Closkey
  M., 31
M'Clung
  J. A., 68, 93
  John A., 41, 61
  Mr., 47, 105
  S., Mrs., 41
M'Connell
  Hugh, 41
M'Cord
  George W., 122
M'Culloch
  Peter, 39
M'Curdy
  Martha, 38
M'Dowell
  S.C.P., Miss, 120
M'Gallaird
  seph, 3
M'Ilvain
  J. B., 48, 60
M'Kibben
  J. T., 51
M'Kinney
  Capt., 44
M'Knon
  John, 41
M'Laughlin

Butcher and M'Laughlin, 97
M'Millin
  Jas., 101
M'Murtrie
  H., 38
  Henry, 36
Machir
  Henry, 9
Mackey
  Jane, 21
  W. M., 57
  William, 21, 25, 71
  Wm., 66, 105, 112
Malay
  Geo. W., Rev., 109
Maltby
  H., 113
  I., 113
Mannen
  J., Col., 31
  John, 34
  John, Col., 31
Maple
  David, 41
  George, 41
Mark
  E., 123
Markham
  Wm., Capt., 103
Markland
  M., 65, 68, 71, 73, 83
  Matthew, 66, 83
Marshall
  Charles A., 81
  Charles T., 34
  George, 124
  George H., 124
  H., 107
  John, 46
  Mr., 100
  Nelson, 68

Reuben, 41
Thomas, 46
Thos., Maj., 41
Marston
  L., 74
Martin
  Jeremiah, 41
Mason
  Elder G., 88
  George, 24
  Stephen T., 100
  William, 41
Massie
  Ann, 45
  Eliza, 45
  Henry, 45
  Nathaniel, 45
  Richard, 45
Masterson
  John, 97
Matchet
  John, 48, 90
Mathews
  Edwin, 41
Mattony
  Richard, 46
Maupin
  R.D., 20
Maxey
  Benjamin, 10
Maxwell
  Maxwell &
    Buchanan, 69
May
  Patrick, 41
Mayer
  B. P., 86
Mayhugh
  Ann, 73
Maysville Auxiliary
  Colonization
  Society, 20
Maysville Thespian
  Society, 3
McAdow
  Sam., 32
McCann

The Maysville Eagle
  Ben., 112
McCardle
  Mr., 58
  W. H., 56
McCauley
  Samuel, 75
McCullough
  Hugh, 68
McIivain
  Jno. B., 73
McIlvain
  Hugh, 80, 118
  Jno. B., 114
  John B., 90, 101, 115
McIlvaine
  Jno., 69
  John B., 112
McIntire
  Alex., 27
McIvain
  Jno. B., 66
McKee
  George R., 86
McKenny
  J. Smith, 71
McKim
  W.M., 103
McKinney
  A. M. Dr., 76
  Daniel, 17
  William, 17
McKinsey
  Thomas, 41
McIvain
  Jno. B., 67
McMillen
  James, 118
McMillin
  Ja's, 98
McNeil
  Capt., 44
  James, 104
Meads
  Leonard, 29
Medaugh
  Nathl., 41

Meenach
  James, 41
Mefford
  George, 110
Mendell
  Thomas &
    Mendell,, 67
Metcalfe
  Artus &
    Metcalfe, 73, 110, 116
  E. F., 54
  Eli F., 118
  Hiram, 50
  John P., 72
  Thomas, Gen., 20, 30, 41, 99
  Thos. Gen., 31
  William, 118
Middleswarth
  Jesse, 41
Milbourn
  James, 28
Miley
  George, 52
Miller
  Achetbeth, 41
  Moses L., 44
Miner
  Miner &
    Cruttenden, 110
Mitchell
  Charles S., 72
  John, 33
  Richard, 46
  Wm., 83
  Wm. R., 83
Mocklar
  Wm. B., 85
Moffett
  J. B., Dr., 124
Moffitt
  Thomas, 108
Montjoy
  Capt., 118
Moody

The Maysville Eagle

Rebecca, 46
Mooklar
  Willaim B., 113
Moore
  Edward, 3
  G. G., Rev., 92
  J. Capt., 52
Moorhead
  Thomas, 77
More
  Benjamin, 41
Morgan
  Daniel, 10
  John S., 103, 124
Morris
  David, 41
  James, 20
  Manual, 39
  W. V., 74
Morrison
  David, 46
  James Morrison
    & Co., 9
  James N., 57, 66, 82
  Jas. N., 57
Morrow
  Thomas, 124
Mortan
  Mortan &
    Proctor, 57
Mortimore
  John, 41
Morton
  Hixson, Morton
    & Hixson, 8
  John, 64
  John M., 57
  Jonathan, 28
  Letitia, 64
  Morton, Proctor
    & Co, 58
  Mr., 49
Moss
  James W., 17
Mower
  Jacob, 41

Murphy
  William, 42
  Wm., 7
Musick
  H.G., 118
Myers
  Allen, 109
  Jacob, 63
Nancy
  John, 41
Nash
  Jesse, 41
  John, 42
  Mary, Mrs., 42
Negro, 34
  Aaron, 76
  Berry, 108
  Boy, 67
  Caleb, 108
  Frank, 108
  Harry, 22
  Henry, 63
  Isaiah, 122
  John, 72
  Kelly, 76
  Lewis, 52
  Littleton, 108
  Nelson, 63
  Peter, 96, 108
  Pompey, 74
  Reuben, 34
  Woman, 27, 53, 97
  Woman & two
    children, 41
  Woman and two
    children., 46
  Negroes, 6, 21, 76, 80, 97, 110, 112
  man, woman and
    child, 112
Nelson
  Doctor, 7
  Dr., 68
  Morgan, 29
  Simon, 85
  T. H., 94

  Thomas H., 94
  Thomas W., 32
New Years Ball., 105
Newdigate
  Wm. C., 50
Newland
  Silas, 108
Newsum
  William, 41
Nicholas
  James, 50
Nicholsen
  Thomas, Capt., 20
Nicholson
  S.B., 84
  Thos., 23
Noble
  Mr., 43
Nolin
  Nolin & Bascom, 80
Norris
  Benj. Capt., 30
  Benjamin, Capt., 30
Norton
  Hiram, 103
  Mrs., 66
O'Bannon
  Emily D., 106
O'Conner
  Jas, Judge, 71
  Susan E., 71
O'Cull
  James, 46
Odd Fellows, 92
Ogden
  Samuel C., 56
Ogdon
  Benjamin, 111
Oliver
  Presley, 123
Oneil
  Elizabeth, 46
O'neil
  Elizabeth, 46

Orr
  Alexander D., 46
  Alexander D., Col., 45
Orsler
  Joseph, 41
Ortkeiss
  Henry, 41
Outten
  Isaac, 20
  Jacob, Jr., 85
Owens
  Augustine C., 63
  Conquest, 50
  Dr., 47
  Ludwell, 1
Pague
  Robert, Gen., 21
Palmer
  Philip, 46
Parish
  John, 45
Parker
  Danl., 42
  Parker & Sharp, 60
  Thomas, 17
  W. B., 92
  William, 19
  William B., Esq., 2
  William W., 100
  Winslow, 6
  Wm., 53
  Wm. Buck, 123
  Wm. S., 1
Parsons
  Gen., 2
Patton
  W. W., Rev., 124
Paxton
  John, 4
Payne
  Duval, Col., 32
  Geo. M., Dr., 41
  John, 3
  John G., 124

The Maysville Eagle
  John N., 46
  Payne & Waller, 119
  Robert, 41, 47, 124
  Tho. Y., 68, 84
  Thomas, 46
  Thomas Y., 32, 63, 83, 102, 118
  Tho's Y., 49
  Thos. Y., 57, 105
Pearce
  H. P., 68, 69
  H. T., 91, 105, 116
  L. C., 68, 91, 116
  Lewis C., 69
  Messrs. Pearce, Fant & Brodrick, 83
  Will., 6
Peck
  A.J., Dr., 31
Peddleord
  Caleb, 41
Peers
  H. P., 67
  H. P., 67, 73
  Val., 6, 24
  Val. Maj., 20
Pemberton
  James, 41
Penn
  Mr., 100
Pepper
  E. S., 124
  William H., 17
Perrine
  Daniel, 4
  G., 4
Perry
  E. R., 116
  Lewis, 56
Peterson
  Wm. S., 29
Phillips

Edmund, 24
James, 55
Mary Ellen, 106
Phillips, Reynolds & Co, 83
W.B., 57
William, 4, 124
Wm. B., 8, 64
Phister
  Charles, 107
  E. C., 94
Pickerel
  James, 124
Pickett
  Doctor, 49
  Ellen, 55
  James C., Col., 55
  John Col., 46
Pilkington
  Samuel, 41
Pindell
  Dr., 43
Piper
  James, 38
Plank
  James C., 124
Plummer
  Eli, 42
  Hirma, 109
Poage
  William I., 65
Pointer
  Elias, 42
Pollard
  Benjamin, 41
Porter
  Charles, 103
  Thomas, 53
Post
  James, Dr., 9
Postlethwait
  John, Capt., 43
Potter
  W.W., **36**
Poyntz

The Maysville Eagle

Mr., 34
N., 52, 91, 96
Nat, 40
Nat., 73, 105
Nathan, 63
W & N, 67
W & Nat., 67
W., 52, 91, 96
W. & Nat., 67
William, 63
Wm., 96
Wm. M., 57, 71, 83
Prather
  John O., 93
Price
  A.E., 43
Procter
  G. M., 67, 69
  Geo. M., 67
  George M., 83
  John N., 124
  L. J., 68
Proctor
  Mortan & Proctor, 57
  Morton, Proctor & Co, 58
Purtee
  James, 106
Quinn
  Aaron, 8
Qutten
  Isaac, 20
  Issac, 8
Rain
  Samuel, 36
Rains
  Henry, 42
Rammelsberg
  Jones & Rammelsberg, 95
Ramy
  Deborah, 46
Randel
  John, 33

Randolph
  Mr., 3
Rankin
  S., 79
Rankins
  B. H., 31
  John, 43, 46
Rannells
  C.S., 62
  Dr., 62
Raulston
  John M., 42
Rector
  Mrs., 21
Redden
  James, Sr., 63
Reed
  Hannah, 16
  John C., 71, 82, 118
  Lewis E., 16
  Richard, 85
Reeder
  Coburn & Reeder, 110, 116
  H. R., 90
Rees
  Rees & Allen, 90, 116, 118
  W., 50, 56
Reeve
  Benj. F., 30
  Benjamin F., 29, 30, 43
  Benjamin, Capt., 30
Reeves
  S., 42
Reid
  J. R., 68
  John C., 64
  Judge, 63
  Walker, 24, 45
Respess
  A. C., 71
Reynolds

B. B., 67, 74
Benj., 83
G. Y., 97
Phillips,
  Reynolds & Co, 83
Rhodes
  Anthony, 104
Rice
  N. L. Rev., 113
  Wm. H., 21
Richardson
  Sarah, 56
  Thomas F., 59
Richart
  Wm., 103
Richeson
  Jno. H., 113, 114
Richey
  William, 26
Ricketts
  R. C., Rev., 106
  Richard C., 119
  T. K., 121
Rideout
  John, 26
  Mr., 26
Rist
  Elizabeth D., 46
Robb
  Joseph, 24, 63
  Maj., 43
  W. W., 73
Robertson
  Dr., 70
  Edward, 46
  Thos. R, 83
  W. H., Dr., 60
Robinson
  Thomas, 44
Rochester
  Judge, 30, 44
  W.B., 44
  W.R., Hon., 43
Rock
  A. W., 122
Roe

The Maysville Eagle

John, 7, 19
Roeby
  Aquiea, 103
Rogers
  B.F., 103
  H. A., 103
  John, 63
  Lewis, 103
  Nathaniel P., 103
  W. S., 103
  Warren B., 103
Roper
  E., 46
Ross
  Jas., 124
  Jonston, 118
  Lewis D., 65
Rothe
  Jno. W., 22
Rudd
  Thomas, Capt., 25
Rudolph
  Tobias, 26
Rumford
  Elizabeth, 42
  Joseph, 51
Runyon
  Asa R., 1
  Dan'l, 111
  Jas. M., 20
Rushton
  Richard K., 42
Russell
  Mr., 86
Ryan
  Charles B., 83
  Cks. B., 108
  Clarke & Ryan, 58
  H. M., 56
  Mr., 58
Saffern
  James, 45
Salisbury
  John, 100
  Thomas, 100

Sampson
  Nathan, 60
  Wm. S., 109, 110, 122
Samuel
  Churchill, 71
Sanders
  George, Sr., 124
Sandford
  Charles, 106
Sanford
  Messrs., 115
Saunders
  Benjamin, 124
Savage
  F. A., 78
  James, 18
  John P., 63
Scott
  James, 42
  Willoughby, 103
Scrogin
  Robert, 20
Scudder
  Charles, 89
Seaton
  A. Dr., 72
  A., Doct., 70
  Dr., 68
  Dr. A., 84
  Seaton & Sharp, 109
  Seaton & Sharpe, 101, 111
  Seaton & Sharpe, 116
Secrest
  Joseph, 20
Seddon
  W. F., 107
Sell
  E. M., 100, 108
servant
  female, 69
  Female, 69
  girl, 69
  Woman, 107

Servant, 121
Shacklefold
  Jno., 71
Shackleford
  Doct., 7
  Dr., 94, 107
  Dr. J., 118
  J., 121
  John, 46
  John, Doctor, 51
Shaddows
  Edward, 42
Shanks
  Family, 11
Sharp
  Parker & Sharp, 60
  Seaton & Sharp, 109
Sharpe
  Kirk, Anderson & Sharpe, 78
  Sam'l K., 105
  Seaton & Sharpe, 101, 111
Shawnees, 2
Shelton
  Austin, 18
  Dabney, 18
  Henry, 18
  John, 18
  Thomas, 18
  William, 18
Shepard
  Chaun., Capt., 42
Shepherd
  Thos. W., 102, 103
Shinn
  Francis, 46
Shockley
  S., 102
Shotwell
  Jabes, 16
  John, 16
  Nathan, 16
Shropshire

The Maysville Eagle

S. G., 105
Shultz
  C., 52, 118
  Christian, 40, 54, 66, 83
  Cleaney & Shultz, 59
Sibbald
  G., 76
Sidener
  Jacob, 97
Simpson
  French, 103
  Jonathan, 20
  Robert, 104
Sinclair
  Geo. H., 42
  George H., 18
Slack
  Jacob, 15
slave
  Harry, 22
Slave holders, 30
slaves, 45
Sloan
  Wm. C., 65
Smather
  R., 46
Smith
  E. J., 103
  Enoch, 103
  John B., 103
  Margaret, 46
  Smith & Harman, 81
Snidow
  William, 65
Sodusky
  Jacob, 103
Southall
  V. W., 104
Southgate
  Richard H., 56
Soward
  A., 31, 98, 99
  Rich., 4
  William, 72

Spalding
  D., Jr., 85
  Dan'l, 68
  James G., 83
Spencer
  Ezra, 42
  John, 45
  Mary, 45
Squires
  James, 103
  Jas., 103
Sroufe
  Amos, 30
Stamper
  J., Rev., 42
Stanley
  M., 75
Stanton
  R. H., 105
Starr
  Thomas S., 10
Steers
  Thomas, 53
Stephenson
  Presley, 42
Sterne
  Oris, 16
Stewart
  A.P., 29
  James, Sir, 2
  R., 28
  William, 65
Stickney & Co's, 52
Stillwell
  J. D., 119
  Jno. D., 108, 117
  Samuel, 42
  W., 119
  Wm., 108, 117
Stith
  Capt. B.B., 5
  Jane, 20
Stockwell
  Coburn & Stockwell's, 60
Stone

Edward, 103
Strode
  William, 106
Stuart
  Fielding, 104
Sublette
  Milton, 46
Sudduth
  Wm., Gen., 95
Sullivan
  John, 42
  Rodney, 65
Summers
  Jesse, 32
Sumner
  Watson, 9
Sumrall
  John, 29
Sumrall & Adams, 34
Sumrall & Adams, 3
Sutton
  Amos, 124
Swain
  Nelson, 120
Swearingen
  Daniel, 42
Tabb
  John, 46
  L., 100
Taliaferro
  Doctor, 49
Tapp
  Elias, 25
Taylor
  E. W., 99
  Francis, 20
  Geo. H., 57
  H., 47, 68, 89, 93, 105
  J. D., 46
  Jos. Dr., 122
  Milton, 42
  Mr., 61
  R., 99
  Richard, 18
  Robert, 41

Solomon, 100
Taylor & Green, 51
Taylor & Green, 74
Tebbs
  Doctor, 76
  Foushee, 45
  Margaret, 45
  Mary, 45
  Samuel, 45
  Thomas, 45
  Willoughby, 45
Terry
  Crawford, 103
  Jeremiah, 103
Thomas
  Benjamin P., 30
  Ex-Governor, 120
  Jacob, 46
  Moses, 42
  O. H. P., 106
  S.C.P., Mrs, 120
  Thomas & Henry, 119
  Thomas & Mendell,, 67
  W.P., 31
  Wm. P., 60
Thompson
  Eliza, 45
  G.C., Maj., 44
  Isaiah, 7
  James, 80
  John L., 31
  R. W., 94
  William L., 45
Thomson
  Wm. W, 81
Thornley
  Thomas S., 60
Thornton
  Edmund, 23
Threikeld
  Cornelius, 42
Throop

The Maysville Eagle
  Dr., 94
P. Throop & Son, 52
Tiffee
  Sarah, Miss, 42
Tilford
  John, 23
Tinney
  John, 79
Todd
  Robert S., 69
Tolle
  Lewis D., 81
Tomkins
  Thomas, 37
Tomson
  Josith, 42
Toole
  E. A., 78
  H. T., 78
Trimble
  John, 20
Triplett
  Margaret, 45
Trumbo
  Andrew, 26, 27
  Isaac, 26
  Jacob, 27
Tucker
  Eli, 3
Tureman
  E., 61
  Henry, 107
  Joseph F., 1
Turner
  Jesse, 107
  Joshua, 120
Tyler
  Gov., 2
  Senator, 2
Tyson
  Job R., 55
Union Hall, 111
Utery
  David, 27
Vanderen
  Stephen M., 77

Vaughn
  Eli, 42
Vimont
  John S., 73
  Lewis, 73
Vogel
  Mr., 99
  Mrs., 99
Wabash Indians, 1
Waddell
  John T., 5
  Wm. B., 89
Wadsworth
  A. A., 72, 82, 102, 105
  Henry, 102
Walder
  B.E., 74
Waldron
  Jubal, 104
Waler
  H., 68
Walker
  Wm., 124
Waller
  Edw'd, 110
  H., 105
  Henry, 59, 95, 119
  Mr., 105, 120
Wallingford
  A. M., 57
Wallingsford
  John, 46
Walton
  John, 15
  Robert, 28, 46
Ward
  Charles, Captain, 54
Warder
  Walter, 20
  Walter, Rev., 45
Warren
  Thos. T. G, 110
Washington Hotel, 59

Washington Inn, 19
Waters
  R. L., 34
Watkins
  Joseph, 103
Watson
  Joseph, 97
  Zephaniah, 98
Webb
  Jno., 9
Weeden
  O. M., 107
Weedon, 68
Weever
  David A., 48
Weiden
  John, 46
Weirick
  George, 17
  Henry, 16, 17, 68
  R. C., 68
Wells
  John S., 67
  William, 26
  Wm., 27
Wetmore
  C. P., 65
Wheeler
  Eliza, 16
  John, 16
Wherney
  Reason, 65
Whipps
  Samuel, 18
White
  Absalom, 22
  John, Hon., 86, 87
  Thos. H., 118
Wickliffe
  Charles H., 44
Wier
  Joshua, 124
Willett

The Maysville Eagle
Handable, 42
James, 42
Williams
  Alfred M., 105
  David M., 124
  George, 17
  John, 73
  Sam'l, 73
  Samuel, Gen., 103
  Thomas H., 70
  Thos., 51
  William B., 10
Wilson
  Edward, 28
  Elizabeth T., 46
  George, 28
  James P., 124
  James R., 42
  John, Major., 33
  Jos., 103
  Joseph, 103
  Josiah, 46
  Mary, 28
  Michael, 5
  Robert, 51
  Saml., 41
  Samuel O., 103
  Thomas, 28
  William, 33, 39, 51
  Wm. H., 46
Winters
  Joshua, 30
Wise
  H. A., 99
Woman
  Negro, 69
Wood
  Charles A., 42
  Daniel, 42, 46
  David, 46
  Henry W., 88, 101

Jesse, 42
Richard, 46
W. R., 48
William R., 60
William R., Dr., 35
Wm. R., 91
Woodward
  Enos, 26, 46
Wormald
  James, 89, 95
Worthington
  Samuel, Col., 98
  William, 20, 41
Worthington & Anderson, 105
Wright
  Sarah, Miss, 42
Wyatt
  J. J., 124
Wythe
  Captain, 46
Yancy
  Charles, 19
Yateman
  H. L., 124
York
  Co., 71
Yorke
  A. F. & Co., 75
Young
  Asa, Col., 20
  J.B., 89
  J.W., 89
  John C., Dr. Rev., 113
  Nicholas, 27
  Thomas, Capt., 45
  Wm. P., 89
Zane
  Noah, 29

www.ingramcontent.com/pod-product-compliance
Lightning Source LLC
Chambersburg PA
CBHW060030180426
43196CB00044B/2288